RELEASED

D1319936

Schools of Tomorrow—
TODAY!

A REPORT

ON EDUCATIONAL

EXPERIMENTS

LB1026.M88S ST. JOSEPH'S UNIVERSITY STX
Schools of tomorrow—today.
3 9353 00035 4983

Schools of Tomorrow—

TODAY!

by ARTHUR D. MORSE

LB1026
M88S

65136

DOUBLEDAY & COMPANY, INC., GARDEN CITY, NEW YORK

LIBRARY OF CONGRESS CATALOG CARD NUMBER 60–11614
COPYRIGHT © 1960 BY ARTHUR D. MORSE
ALL RIGHTS RESERVED
PRINTED IN THE UNITED STATES OF AMERICA

DESIGN: CHARLES KAPLAN

CONTENTS

Foreword by James E. Allen, Jr.   6

1. *Team Teaching in Action:* THE FRANKLIN SCHOOL OF LEXINGTON, MASS.   9

2. *Schools Without Grades:* THE ELEMENTARY SCHOOLS OF APPLETON, WIS.   27

3. *The Search for Hidden Talent:* NEW YORK CITY'S DEMONSTRATION GUIDANCE PROJECT   41

4. *Freeing the Teacher for Teaching:* THE TEACHER AIDES OF BAY CITY, MICH.   61

5. *Television Pioneer:* WASHINGTON COUNTY, MD.   79

6. *Experiments in Excellence:* EVANSTON (ILL.) TOWNSHIP HIGH SCHOOL. GOLDEN (COLO.) HIGH SCHOOL   101

7. *Breaking the Rural Barrier:* THE CATSKILL PROJECT   123

8. *The Electronic Link:* TELEVISION IN SOUTH-WESTERN INDIANA   143

9. *Teachers of Tomorrow:* THE HARVARD PROGRAM   159

Appendix—Related Experimental Programs

TEAM TEACHING   175

UNGRADED PRIMARY SCHOOLS   176

TEACHER AIDES   178

TELEVISION   179

THE GIFTED CHILD   180

SUMMER PROGRAMS FOR GIFTED STUDENTS   184

IMPROVEMENT OF RURAL SCHOOLS   187

TEACHER RECRUITMENT   189

THE NEW TECHNOLOGY   191

Foreword

AMERICAN EDUCATION IS IN FERMENT. UN-precedented problems of quantity and quality call for unprecedented solutions.

In 1960, 35.3 million boys and girls are registered in the public elementary and secondary schools of this nation. According to estimates of the U.S. Office of Education, their schooling is handicapped by a shortage of about 200,000 teachers and 132,000 classrooms. Compounding the problem, about 11% of the teachers leave their profession each year. So much for the numbers.

Serious questions have arisen regarding the quality of U.S. education. While Soviet scientific progress has provided a catalyst, thoughtful inquiry into methods of improving our system of universal public education long preceded the satellite race. I believe that a concern for broader education in the humanities and social sciences should have as much priority in the schools as the exploration of outer space.

There are obvious defects in a system which prides itself on its democratic character but does not educate youngsters to their fullest capacities. Three of every ten boys and four of every ten girls in the upper quarter of their high school graduating classes do not enter college. This is a tragic national loss at a time when our need for talented manpower is urgent. Apart from the national consequences this is an incalculable personal loss to the families involved.

It seems apparent, therefore, that more than numerical solutions to these problems are demanded. To this end thousands of experimental programs are now under way.

Never before in history have our schools engaged in such widespread experimentation to meet the new educational requirements. Never before have so many hopeful new approaches developed in such a relatively short period. An intense self-examination is now under way on a national scale. In the process we are learning that many of the old ways of operating our schools are not necessarily the best ways. New methods of organization, the use of new technological devices and new concepts of the role of the teacher provide answers that numbers alone cannot provide.

It seemed to me that the teachers, school board members, superintendents, principals and interested lay citizens of New York State should know about these experiments and consider their possible applicability to local situations. My colleagues at the New York State Education Department agreed and we decided that descriptions of some of the more promising experiments should be non-technical, based on personal observation and of practical value to the reader. We found that this material had never been brought together, though snatches had appeared in educational journals and formal reports.

We presented our proposal to the Fund for the Advancement of Education and a grant for the project was made to the Department. To execute the proposal we sought someone not only knowledgeable about current developments in American education but also able to describe the most significant of these developments imaginatively in terms of their promise for general application. We were fortunate in securing Arthur D. Morse, an award-winning educational writer and producer-director of several outstanding television programs.

Mr. Morse's journalism honors include the Freedom Foundation's Award for "Jackie Wouldn't Have Gotten to First Base," (the boyhood of Jackie Robinson, Better Homes and Gardens, 1950); the $500 Sidney Hillman Foundation award, the Sigma Delta Chi annual award "for distinguished public-service journalism" and the Education Writer's Association annual award for "Who's Trying to Ruin Our Schools?" (McCall's, 1952); and the Christophers Award for "Bay City Beats the Teacher Shortage" (Collier's and Reader's Digest, 1956).

Recently Mr. Morse produced and directed the National Education Association's documentary filmed report, "How Good Are Our Schools? Dr. Conant Reports . . . ."

In determining which experiments to include in this volume, Mr. Morse canvassed every State Education Department, invited suggestions from private and governmental organizations, examined the existing literature, studied programs supported by the foundations and sought the advice of many educators.

On the basis of this research he chose ten experiments in eight states and made an intensive first-hand study of these programs. He had complete freedom of selection and worked independently.

The experiments chosen are not panaceas. They are not recommended as the best or the only answers to local problems. They were picked because they represent a cross-section of experimentation, they are in operation *now* and their early results appear to be hopeful.

It is entirely possible that there exist similar and perhaps more effective examples which have not been included. The field is vast and there is much room for individual judgment.

Taken together, the experiments covered in the nine chapters and the capsule descriptions of related programs in the Appendix, cover a wide spectrum of American education. The names of local contacts for each experiment enable readers to obtain additional information.

A high proportion of these experiments were aided by grants from the Ford Foundation and its Fund for the Advancement of Education. This is not surprising because the Fund is oriented toward new developments in this field.

It is encouraging to note the growing activity of other foundations in this area. In the past the public schools have received little support of this type.

In addition to foundation-supported programs, a number of experiments are described which do not involve extra financing or whose costs are borne locally or by state education departments. A local climate in which experimentation can flourish would seem to be a necessity for better schools.

There are many significant advances in education beyond the scope of this book. Their omission is not intended to lessen their distinction. Among these are exciting revisions in curriculum which are being made by some of our most gifted scholars. These deserve future volumes in themselves.

We of the New York State Education Department believe that *Schools of Tomorrow—Today!* presents a vivid picture of the kind of experimentation which promises to lift the level of American education while it helps to solve the critical problems of quantity and quality. We express our thanks to the many people throughout the country who cooperated with Mr. Morse in his research and travels. A special word of acknowledgment is due Miss Elizabeth Sweeney who, as secretary-researcher, made a valuable contribution to this project.

JAMES E. ALLEN, JR.
*Commissioner of Education
and
President of the University
of the State of New York*

March 1, 1960

1. *Team Teaching in Action:*

THE FRANKLIN SCHOOL
OF LEXINGTON, MASS.

THE FLOODTIDES OF SCIENCE, SOCIAL change and world upheaval have had little perceptible effect on the American elementary school.

At age six our youngsters begin an educational lockstep that moves them forward uniformly year after year with little distinction as to differences of ability.

In endless thousands of brick-and-glass buildings they sit in uniform groups of 25 to 35. They remain in the same room virtually the entire day. They receive all their lessons from the same teacher regardless of her strengths and weaknesses.

With equal disregard for differences in ability school boards pay each teacher essentially the same salary. The gifted teacher can improve her status in one way—by taking an administrative position which will shatter the relationship which established her superiority—her contact with students.

Once rooted in a classroom with her 25 to 35 children the typical teacher has little opportunity for professional growth. Her contacts with other teachers are limited. Although she is at school all day she rarely, if ever, observes

11

a superior teacher in action. Part of her day is wasted in nonprofessional, clerical chores. Her creativeness is restricted to one room, one class. Her inabilities are also limited to one room, one class and frequently remain undiscovered. She is an important part of the world of scholarship, but the great universities which dominate that world play no role in her career.

This is a bleak picture of the American elementary school teacher and many efforts are being made to revise this image. One of the most promising is the team teaching experiment in Lexington, Mass.

From the outside Lexington's Franklin School resembles any other elementary school housing 500 youngsters in grades 1 to 6. There the similarity ends.

Franklin's faculty is divided into three teams, Alpha, Beta and Omega. Each is headed by a team leader, a highly gifted and experienced teacher who receives an additional salary of $1,000 a year. Next ranking in the team are senior teachers who have above average competence, possess specialized skills and receive $500 extra. The regular teachers who comprise the bulk of each team earn the same salaries as they would in a conventional Lexington school.

Alpha consists of a team leader, three teachers and 75 first graders. Beta is comprised of a team leader, one senior teacher, five teachers and 187 second and third graders. Omega rounds out the Franklin School teaching teams with a team leader, two senior teachers, five teachers and 230 fourth, fifth and sixth graders. Clerical aides relieve each team of paperwork and secretarial chores.

Directing and evaluating the experiment are members of the School and University Program for Research and

Development. Known as SUPRAD, this organization joins the school systems of Concord, Lexington and Newton, Mass., with Harvard's Graduate School of Education. SUPRAD originated the team teaching concept.

Within the team structure every stereotype and cliché of elementary education is under attack. What happens to Billy, a seven-year-old second grader, can only happen in the Lexington school. For one thing, where else could Billy be a Beta?

Billy and 27 classmates spend the 8:30 to 9 a.m. period in their homeroom, 4A, with Miss Doughty, a brand new teacher. They pledge allegiance and carry out routine chores. At 9, without any bells ringing, youngsters throughout the school "redeploy." This word conjures up armies on the march but the movements are quiet and unregimented.

Billy heads for Room 6A, where his Beta reading group of medium-high ability is scheduled to meet with Miss Levens, the team leader. Other Beta teachers handle separate groups of high, medium-low and low pupils. Their varied teaching techniques have been agreed upon at frequent team meetings.

Some of Billy's homeroom friends are in Miss Levens' class but that's only because their reading ability at the moment is on his level. With team teaching Billy can look forward to new acquaintances in each room.

There are 35 students in Billy's reading group but the Franklin teachers are not obsessed by "magic numbers." They recognize that some subjects can be taught successfully to 200 students, others to fewer than 15. Team teaching permits this flexibility.

At 10 a.m., Billy returns to his homeroom for the inevitable milk and crackers and after a short stint on the playground joins 90 Betas in the cafeteria—for penmanship.

Mrs. Sullivan teaches handwriting skills to her 90 pupils by means of an overhead projector. She places her paper at the correct slant on the projector and its magnified image covers the cafeteria wall. Her hand and her pencil are enlarged enormously as she shapes the letters on the paper. The words fill the cafeteria wall. Billy and his Beta friends see them more clearly than if they were written on a classroom chalkboard.

As she writes Mrs. Sullivan speaks softly into a microphone which carries her words clearly to the large group. She is regarded as an excellent teacher but she would be disqualified by most school systems. As a mother of two small children she can teach only half a day. Schools which require each teacher to instruct a single class in all subjects for a full day would not hire her. In spite of the acute teacher shortage her talents would be wasted.

In Lexington's team teaching plan there is room for part-time teachers. Because Mrs. Sullivan directs the penmanship practice of 90 children, half the teachers of the Beta team are freed for the planning and preparation of other lessons. This is an opportunity denied to the typical elementary teacher.

At 11 o'clock, Mrs. Sullivan turns off the projector. It is time for another redeployment. Billy packs away his penmanship paper which is covered with crisply written Halloween words and heads for Room 8A and arithmetic. His arithmetic level, unlike his reading level, is medium-low and his class is smaller.

Ability grouping in a conventional elementary school divides youngsters into gifted, average or slow homeroom units and assumes that this pattern holds true in all subjects. Team teaching recognizes that ability in language arts may not insure equal ability in number concepts. At the Franklin School children and their parents are not as conscious of an ability "niche" because the students find themselves in different company in each class.

At 11:50, Billy returns to his homeroom and prepares for lunch. He eats from 12 to 12:30, after which he has 20 minutes of physical education. Here his teacher is talented Temple Fawcett, a senior teacher in music, art and physical education who serves each of the three teams. Unlike the typical elementary school whose classroom teachers are expected to carry music, art and physical education programs with occasional help from visiting specialists, Franklin School provides continuing programs directed by Miss Fawcett.

Like most Franklin teachers her summer work relates directly to the following year's program. Continuing graduate courses at Boston University last summer she wrote, "I hope to be able to build a number of lessons or units where art and music can be integrated and to tie in such physical education activities as folk dancing and singing games."

She has achieved this objective in many ways. This year she staged a lecture-demonstration on ballads for 150 Omega pupils. After introducing folk music in an auditorium lecture she enrolled students in one of five groups exploring the subject. One group painted murals illustrating the ballads. A creative writing group developed tall stories based on the themes, choral and dramatization

15

groups offered ancient and modern versions and the music group made up new lyrics to familiar tunes.

But back to Billy. It is now 12:50, he has been physically educated and he must return to his homeroom to prepare for his next move. At 1 p.m. he returns to Miss Levens' class for the social studies portion of his language arts studies.

In Miss Levens Billy has a teacher expert in subject matter as well as in educational theory. She was chosen to head her team because her 10 years of teaching had revealed inescapable qualities of leadership. Having obtained her master's degree from Harvard's Graduate School of Education she is now completing requirements for her doctorate.

This year Miss Levens' team decided to avoid the "smattering of information" approach to social studies. For farming, one of the major topics, each chose an area of concentration.

Miss Levens boned up on the subject, "How soil determines what is raised locally." Other teachers singled out weather effects on soil, regional and national factors in crop growth and area influences in lumbering. This sharp focus is of benefit to Billy and all Betas as well as to new teachers like Cynthia Landauer.

Mrs. Landauer is a member of Miss Levens' team. A 1956 graduate of Radcliffe with a major in anthropology and a candidate for Harvard's master of arts in teaching, she is known as an intern teacher.

"I get so much more help than other beginning teachers," she reports. "I know that if it weren't for the team setup I'd have that sense of loneliness that every inexperienced teacher has behind the closed doors of her classroom. The members of my team are friendly and eager to help. There's a constant exchange of ideas about the children. We have a chance to pool our knowledge about them."

Large group lessons and flexible scheduling free the team leaders for planning and supervision. Miss Levens has one full day and two mornings free for observing Mrs. Landauer and other Beta teachers in action. In addition she links the team by a stream of conferences and memos.

Here are brief excerpts from recent notes she has circulated:

Parent Conferences

Each team member has been assigned a week in which to initiate conferences. Other team members participate if necessary.

Think-abouts

Handwriting: Lois is interested in handwriting—how can we change the schedule to make use of her interest?

Art: Are the periods too short? What are the possibilities for hour-long periods?

Rainy Mornings: Can we smooth out the details of what the children do when teachers have meetings on rainy days?

Music: Helen said she has taken large group music with camp groups. Can we plan some time for her to sing with several groups at a time?

Creative Writing: Teddi always does such a magnificent job in creative writing. Can't we arrange a series of large groups for her to be in charge of for other classes? (providing she's willing, naturally)

In the traditional elementary school this interchange of ideas is virtually impossible. Teachers tend to work separately.

This constant exchange of views strengthens the Beta team. For Billy at the moment it means carefully planned lessons on farming.

At 2:50 p.m., bursting with information about the soil of Lexington, he leaves Miss Levens' class and returns to his homeroom for dismissal for the day. His busy day and exposure to many adults contrasts sharply with the routine of typical second graders throughout the United States.

The team teachers of Lexington, like educators involved in other promising experiments, are discovering that youngsters are more flexible, mature and reliable than is generally realized. Taboos which have persisted throughout the years because of unsupported theories are tumbling in all directions. For example, the same day that Billy made his rounds of Beta, the 75 first graders of Alpha assembled for a science lesson. The subject: sound.

Few schools would dare to present such a topic to six-year-olds. Fewer would attempt it with such a large group and fewer still would expect that the children's interest could be sustained for 40 minutes.

Introducing the role of the senses, the science teacher asked the first graders why smell was important.

"Because," chirped a voice, "it helps me like my breakfast before I come downstairs."

Having thus established the scientific significance of

18

smell, the teacher proceeded to other senses including hearing. She explained that sound is caused by vibrations and she struck tuning forks, jingled bells under water and made the air hum with assorted quivering noises. Within minutes the class had mastered "vibration"—the word and the concept.

Happily noting their riveted attention, the teacher ignored textbook maxims about the inevitability of restlessness and continued her demonstrations with a slight pause for the class to rise and stretch.

After 40 minutes she asked, "How many boys and girls would like to talk about sound another day?"

Every hand was raised. Then the six-year-olds broke up into small groups and without apparent traumatic effects filed quietly into other rooms for other subjects.

Merrel Collard, team leader of Omega which includes fourth, fifth and sixth graders, notes the same eagerness among the older students. He supervises a group of eight gifted arithmetic students who are doing high school work in the sixth grade. They have laid out a playground, blueprinted alterations to a house and researched number systems. Their program includes mastery of the slide rule. Collard gives them freedom for self-direction and they work unstintingly whether he is in the room or not. Another Omega advanced arithmetic class consists of 1 fourth grader, 5 fifth graders and 15 sixth graders, a grouping impossible in the conventional school with its rigid grade levels.

In another example of grade crossing, Omega's most highly skilled remedial reading teacher gives individualized instruction to less advanced fourth, fifth and sixth graders in the same room.

Mrs. Ethel Bears has been principal of Franklin School since the team teaching experiment was inaugurated in 1957. Her unruffled disposition and flexibility account in large part for the smooth transition to team teaching.

"This has been a very exciting experience," she says. "Many of our preconceived notions have been swept out from under us. As a result we find teaching more rewarding. Our constant contact with Harvard University, which made this program possible, adds a new stimulation to the life of this school."

The Lexington experiment stems in part from a proposal made to the Fund for the Advancement of Education in April 1956 by Dean Francis Keppel of Harvard's Graduate School of Education. It is a relentlessly analytical look at some of the inadequacies of American education. Excerpts, while not doing it complete justice, may reveal some of its highlights.

"The plain fact," wrote Dean Keppel, "is that the higher institutions of learning have not fulfilled their responsibility or met the new challenge of matching performance with ideas in public education . . . Major changes in the policies and organization of American public education are required . . . The first step is a clarification of the role of the university in relation to public education. From this will follow, we believe, a new pattern of cooperation between universities and school systems . . . they must establish relations with schools analogous to those long in effect between medical schools and hospitals.

"Scholarship and research," continued Dean Keppel, "are traditionally areas assigned to the university of our society. So too is the recruitment, selection and training of leaders for the professions . . . Not enough young people are entering teaching and the quality of many of those who do is inadequate. The schools of education and teachers colleges do not have a good record in competition with other professions . . . The programs we propose will require the cooperation of faculty members from many parts of the university: of scholars from the arts, social sciences, physical sciences and medicine, as well as from education."

The Dean pointed out that almost 10 percent of U.S. teachers leave the profession each year, that at any given time half the American children are being taught by relatively inexperienced teachers, over 80 percent of whom are observed by supervisors less than once a month.

"The time has come," wrote Dean Keppel, "to recognize the difference between those who make a lifetime career in education and those who stay only a few years, or who teach part-time . . . At present organizational patterns treat all alike. So do university and college programs of preparation."

Dean Keppel pointed out that unlike careers in business, law and government the teaching profession is characterized by "lack of advancement . . . lack of a sense of goal, absence of increased responsibility and opportunity to use special abilities which usually accompany merit and experience . . . Salaries are not only too low—they also do not offer any range. They seem to operate on the assumption that all teachers are the same and all teaching jobs alike."

Dean Keppel then outlined the structure of the teaching teams as they were later to be formed at Lexington.

"The temper of the times," he concluded, "seems to be right for experimentation and innovation in education."

21

Dean Keppel's proposal resulted in a grant from the Fund for the Advancement of Education for the establishment of SUPRAD. In addition to team teaching at Lexington, there are other SUPRAD programs in the school systems of Concord and Newton, Mass. Each of these experiments is designed to narrow the gap between research and practice by linking the university with public school systems to make teaching more attractive and effective and to extend the influence of gifted teachers.

SUPRAD's project director for the Franklin School experiment is Dr. Robert H. Anderson, associate professor of education at the Graduate School and director of its teacher training programs for elementary schools.

Dr. Anderson has an eloquent capsule description of the experiment.

"We are questioning the status quo," he explains.

The SUPRAD office at the Franklin School maintains constant liaison with the teaching staff and helps to direct the development and research of the experiment. SUPRAD personnel are extremely conservative about the early results of team teaching. They are convinced, on the basis of achievement tests and of comparisons between Franklin youngsters and a control group, that academic results were at least as good as under the traditional system. SUPRAD states that Franklin School youngsters "were in no way confused or caused to be emotionally disturbed by the new program."

SUPRAD believes that "pupil enthusiasm has increased," that early results indicate that elementary school students can be instructed "in groups two to six times the usual class size on appropriate occasions" and that teachers are able to adjust to new working conditions more easily "than is customarily assumed by research workers."

Franklin School parents and children are much freer in their praise of team teaching than the cautious officials of SUPRAD.

Two hundred forty-seven parents attending a parent-teacher association meeting responded to a questionnaire asking their opinions of the experiment.

The following are the responses to two key questions concerning their evaluation of the child's enjoyment of the program and their opinion of its effectiveness. Percentages of parents responding are listed under each grade:

	GRADES					
CHILD ENJOYS	1 %	2 %	3 %	4 %	5 %	6 %
very much	63.4	60.0	58.2	50.0	50.0	45.1
enjoys	23.0	38.6	33.2	50.0	36.8	35.4
neutral	7.7	3.2	5.5	0.0	10.5	19.3
dislikes	3.8	0.0	0.0	0.0	0.0	0.0
miserable	0.0	0.0	2.8	0.0	0.0	0.0
no response	1.9	0.0	0.0	0.0	2.6	0.0

COMPARATIVE EFFECT

	1	2	3	4	5	6
very beneficial	44.2	35.4	27.7	28.6	28.9	41.9
beneficial	23.0	32.2	44.3	50.0	47.3	38.6
about the same	5.8	24.2	13.9	17.9	15.8	9.7
harmful	1.9	0.0	2.8	0.0	0.0	0.0
very harmful	0.0	0.0	0.0	0.0	0.0	0.0
no response	25.0	8.4	11.1	3.6	7.9	9.7

The children of the Franklin School are more articulate than either their parents or the experts of SUPRAD about the benefits of team teaching. Here are comments from fifth and sixth graders:

"You can't get stuck with a boring teacher because now you've got a couple of teachers." . . . "I meet kids on my own level. If I'm a genius the other kids understand me. If I'm not very smart they'll understand me too." . . . "You get more teacher opinions and you learn to get along with them all—the ones who like you to argue and the ones who don't." . . . "Arithmetic is much better now. We have team-work with partners. If you have trouble you're allowed to discuss it with your partner. We're treated more like grownups" . . . "If you're in a low language arts class you can work up to a medium or high group." . . . "Mr. —— tells us not to be afraid to argue with him. He says we have to learn critical thinking and we have debates and we act as reporters and get people's opinions and do so many things to get us ready for high school."

Perhaps the most eloquent evidence of the success of the Lexington experiment is the fact that the community has taken steps to construct a new elementary school designed specifically for team teaching. This means the availability of flexible-size areas for large and small-group lessons and independent study. Movable room dividers will help to make this possible.

Franklin School teachers agree that certain classes in the perceiving phases of learning—listening, reading and watching—lend themselves to large groups. These can range from 75 to 200 students. Other classes, which involve give and take between pupils or between pupils and teachers, as in recitation and discussion, are best suited to smaller groups than the 30–35 of conventional schools. The most desirable number may be 10 students or less. Team teaching makes both extremes possible.

As a SUPRAD report points out, "Conventionally constructed school buildings with their rows of equally sized, self-contained cells divided by immovable partitions do not meet the needs of most effective team operation."

Although the new building will feature versatility it will cost approximately the same as a traditional school. But team teaching, with its upgraded salary scales, is likely to add 10 to 15 percent to the cost of operating the school. Taxpayers in other communities will have to determine whether the apparent advantages to their youngsters are worth this added expense. Meanwhile SUPRAD and the faculty of Franklin School will pursue the goals that dollars and cents cannot obscure—a higher standard of teaching leading to a higher standard of education.

> For further information about Team Teaching in Lexington, contact:
>
> > SUPRAD
> > Harvard University
> > Graduate School of Education
> > Lawrence Hall, Kirkland St.
> > Cambridge 38, Mass.
>
> For a related experimental program see Appendix, p. 175.

2. *Schools Without Grades:*

THE ELEMENTARY SCHOOLS
OF APPLETON, WIS.

Team teaching at the Franklin School of Lexington, Mass., represents one new approach to elementary education—the ungraded primary school represents another.

Ungraded primary schools seek to liberate children from the tyranny of grade levels, permitting them to move ahead in accordance with their individual abilities.

Many communities have experimented in the partial ungrading of elementary schools. Total ungrading has occurred in Appleton, Wis.

THERE ARE NO FIRST, SECOND, THIRD, fourth, fifth or sixth grade pupils in the elementary schools of Appleton, Wis. Children are ungraded. They are neither promoted nor failed. They do not receive report cards.

Under Appleton's Continuous Progress Plan, youngsters move along as fast as their individual abilities can take them. Free from the artificial limits of grade requirements they push on beyond these arbitrary boundaries. In the process they meet the toughest competitive challenge in the world—the challenge to achieve their highest capacity.

Appleton, a city of 50,000, has made a start in breaking the chronological lockstep in education. Its school administration has not been content with platitudes.

For years educators have hailed the doctrine of individual differences between children. It has been widely accepted that boys and girls progress at different rates of speed with bursts of achievement followed by interludes of apathy.

Dean Willard C. Olson of the University of Michigan has put it succinctly: ". . . individual differences in children are lawful expressions of designs for growing."

Though educators have paid lip service to this point of view they have continued to lump individuals together on the basis of age. The first-graders line up at the starting point at age six regardless of maturity or ability and march together year after year with little regard for their uniqueness as individuals. Ability grouping provides in some degree for these differences but grade levels are rigid structures which do not topple regardless of talent.

In many schools children who have completed curriculum requirements before the end of the year are not allowed to progress beyond their grade. This kind of progress complicates matters for next year's teacher, the school principal and the librarian. Life is simpler for the administrator when children move forward with chronological uniformity.

The "pass or fail" pressures of the September to June grade system have long seemed unhealthy to many educators. A slow-starter may receive an unwarranted brand as a failure and an *A,B,C,D* type of report card may reveal nothing of the individual's capabilities.

Appleton's Continuous Progress Plan breaks with the traditions of September to June, "pass or fail" and uniformity. It is moving slowly toward eliminating age barriers but rapidly toward respect for individual differences. The homegrown plan, executed at no additional cost, is disarmingly simple.

After one year of kindergarten, children enter primary school for a three-year program. They are not given grade labels but are expected to complete an impressive academic program during the three-year bloc. Parents are informed about their children's strengths and weaknesses during a minimum of two parent-teacher conferences and by a midyear progress report. The progress report lists no numerical or alphabetical marks and contains no endless checklists of social and emotional characteristics. It describes with clarity the childs' performance in relation to his capacity.

After completing three years of primary school, the Appleton youngster begins three years of intermediate school. A continuing battery of achievement tests enables the teacher to pinpoint the child's accomplishments and failings at parent-teacher conferences. During the final year of intermediate school the student participates in these conferences.

Most youngsters enter junior high school after this seven-year period but those who reveal immaturity or academic deficiencies may remain in either the primary or intermediate bloc for an extra year. Usually the decision to spend the extra year is made before the end of the term to lessen its impact on the child. Teachers discuss this with both the parents and the children.

Under Continuous Progress less than one-half of 1 percent of the students remain an additional year. Before the plan went into effect, Appleton's failure rate under the conventional graded system ranged from about 5 percent in the 1922–35 period to about 2 percent in 1951.

Does this mean that Appleton children are being coddled, that they are not being prepared for the realities of life?

According to standardized achievement tests they are outperforming their predecessors in graded classes and are exceeding national norms in all subjects.

In 1958 intermediate students made higher scores in the California Achievement Tests in reading, arithmetic and language arts than the Appleton youngsters of 1948. What's more, the level seems to be rising.

In 1956 children in their first year of intermediate school exceeded the national norm in total achievement by six months. In 1957 the same group increased its margin to seven months and in 1958, before entering junior high school, they were a full year and one month above the national median.

Appleton's respect for individual differences begins before a child reaches kindergarten age. Children whose fifth birthday occurs before September 1 enter kindergarten automatically, but special provision is made for advanced youngsters with September, October and November birthdays. Parents are notified that these underage children are eligible for testing to determine whether they are ready for school. The tests are not mandatory and some parents prefer to wait the extra year. In 1959, 227 youngsters were examined and 106 were accepted for early admission to kindergarten.

Followup studies of the young entrants of the past reveal their high performance. Twenty-nine of the 46 early admission students completing Appleton elementary schools in 1959 ranked in the first of four reading groups; 10 were in the second; 7 in the third; none in the fourth.

Appleton youngsters attend conventional sized classes and their self-contained classrooms are of the familiar pattern. When schools have more than one class of the same level, students are grouped according to maturity. They may be shifted from one room to another during the year. Within each room they are divided again into small groups for reading, spelling and arithmetic. Each child has his individual skill card.

The skill card is a four-page folder on which the child's scholastic progress is charted. It breaks down arithmetic skills to be mastered during the six years of primary and intermediate school but there are no target dates listed. Entries are made by teachers when the skill is first introduced and later mastered. There are similar sections in reading and spelling. The skill card, a vivid picture of continuous progress, is passed from teacher to teacher until the youngster reaches junior high school. At the beginning of each new term the teacher simply picks up where her predecessor ended.

Appleton teachers and principals are discovering the same delightful truths that characterize experimentation all over the United States. When children and teachers are free to probe beyond limits established by administrative convenience, their potential soars.

There is a boy at the Foster School who read fluently while in kindergarten. When he began primary school his advanced reading status did not embarrass his teacher. She has assigned him responsibilities which put his talent to work without singling him out obtrusively. Periodically he reads a list of books lent to his class by the public library and collects them for return.

When he brought a caterpillar to class his teacher assigned him to find and read a book describing the development of butterflies and moths.

This boy is not held back because the rest of the class has not yet learned to read. On the other hand, he is not pushed ahead on all fronts.

"He is immature in many ways," says his teacher, "and he wants to remain with his group. His arithmetic concepts are not advanced and he's uncomfortable with older boys

33

and girls. Six or seven other children are developing reading skills rapidly and eventually he'll have plenty of companionship. Meanwhile he's moving ahead with his reading without being segregated from his friends."

Asked about her reaction to Continuous Progress, she replied, "I think it's wonderful psychologically. I'm not conscious of June any more as the month that spells success or failure. We're concerned about progress during a three-year period, not about the ups and downs of a child's schooling during the next few months. The skill cards enable us to give new work to the advanced youngsters instead of 'busy work' to fill the time until the slower children catch up."

Youngsters who are ready for work beyond primary school level are encouraged to tackle intermediate subjects. A group of primary boys and girls at Huntley School who had read more than 30 books listed on their skill cards completed as many as 50 additional volumes in early 1959. This self-selection process, which is encouraged in all Appleton schools, is designed to stimulate self-direction and a sense of discovery. In November 1959 the group began reading intermediate material although they do not become intermediates officially until September 1960.

The same is true in arithmetic. Twelve Huntley youngsters, having completed primary work in November 1959 and ranking in the top 10 percent of arithmetic students based on national test results, have launched intermediate work instead of delaying for the starting-gun in September of 1960. When they reach intermediate school their teachers will inherit advanced students with advanced skill cards and there will be no lost motion in discovering their talents.

Discovery is also a keynote of Appleton's parent-teacher conferences. There is nothing unusual about voluntary meetings but Appleton's insistence on a minimum of two conferences a year has proved highly effective. For one thing some parents come to school only when summoned. For another, problems come to light which might never have been recognized.

"There was a boy in my class," a teacher reported recently, "who seemed suddenly to be in a state of shock. He was silent, stared straight ahead, refused to participate in classroom discussions. There was no explanation from home but the boy's mother was due for a regular conference so I didn't contact her. When she came to see me I told her about ——'s sudden change.

" 'Didn't he tell you about his grandfather's death?' she asked. '—— was terribly close to his grandfather because his father travels a great deal and they did many things together while my husband was on the road. When his grandfather died the bottom just dropped out of his world.'

"If it weren't for that meeting with the mother," added the teacher, "I might have pressured —— and it would have been just the wrong thing at that time. If a youngster's parent dies we usually hear of it at school and we're prepared to understand his reaction but other deaths in the family or more subtle matters rarely reach us except at conferences."

Conferences enable teachers to present parents with a realistic picture of their youngsters' attainments at school.

"Profiles" of each child show his standing in reading vocabulary, reading comprehension, arithmetic reasoning, arithmetic fundamentals, mechanics of English and spelling in relation to national norms and the record of his own group. By comparing the child's mental capacity with his actual achievement parent and teacher can see visually whether he is achieving his full capabilities.

The participation of students in the final conference of the intermediate school has proved a great success. It gives them a realistic look at their assets and liabilities as they are about to enter junior high school. Questionnaires were sent to 380 families requesting their reaction to the parent-teacher-child meetings; 272 replied.

> *Question 1.*
>
> Did you like the idea of having your child participate in the final spring conference?
>
> Yes *268;* No *4*
>
> *Question 2.*
>
> Did your child express a willingness to participate in the conference?
>
> Eager *113;* Willing *138;* Indifferent *11;* Reluctant *7;* Unwilling *6*
>
> *Question 3.*
>
> What was your child's reaction following the conference?
>
> Pleased *163;* Enthusiastic *23;* Indifferent *9;* More Informed *97*
>
> *Question 4.*
>
> Do you feel this three-way method of conferring has merit and should be continued as a means of developing mutual understanding?
>
> Yes *265;* No *7*
>
> *Note:*
>
> Some parents checked more than one blank in questions 2 and 3.

Appleton teachers believe that conferences and progress reports provide more meaningful appraisal of a youngster than the naked marks on a report card.

In April 1959 a survey of unsigned teacher opinions revealed that of 73 primary and intermediate teachers who had taught in both *A,B,C* and progress reporting systems, 69 preferred the progress report.

Supporters of progress reporting point out that traditional report cards assume that all children are alike and are striving for the same goals. Adults, they say, never attempt to compare the work of a teacher, a mechanic and a physician, but adherents of numerical or alphabetical marking do not recognize the inborn differences of children.

Report cards purport to be based on a fixed standard but the standards vary from teacher to teacher. Even if the standard is fixed accurately, a "mark" can only compare a youngster to the rest of the group and may have no relation to his potential. The report card, its critics conclude, tends to bring undue pressure on the slower pupils while it fails to challenge the more gifted student.

The Appleton progress report form provides parents with a large space in which to write their comments. A recent examination of hundreds of these statements revealed that fewer than 10 preferred a return to the conventional report card. The opinions of the overwhelming majority are reflected by these two comments:

"You really know our ——! Both of us feel you've 'hit the nail on the head' in most all of your statements. We feel —— is extremely fortunate to have a teacher who knows him well and understands how to cope with his boundless energy . . ."

. . . "We are deeply grateful for the intelligent, sensitive teaching that —— is receiving this year. Surely it reaches far beyond the mechanics of the teaching profession. We know that —— will long remember intermediate I as one of the happiest of all, for it has been a year free of pressure and tension yet one in which he appears to be making steady progress at a healthy rate of speed."

The Continuous Progress Plan is still at an early stage of its development. Its full potential has not been realized and Appleton school officials are the first to point this out. One of the richest possibilities lies in mixed grouping. This would bring together in the same room children of varied ages. Today the bright students forge ahead within the same classroom as less gifted youngsters of the same age. Appleton teachers point out that in many instances this is desirable because the student who is academically advanced may be immature socially and require the companionship of classmates of the same age.

They hasten to add, however, that the fulfillment of their belief that children can proceed at their own pace would be the elimination of arbitrary boundaries between the various years of primary and intermediate school. They accept the fact that many gifted children are mature enough to work with older classmates.

When Appleton solves this problem it will have broken the chronological lockstep completely. At the moment there are 13 "mixed group" classes blending youngsters separated by at least one year of school experience.

At the Edison School a skilled teacher is experimenting with a class containing children of the first and second years of primary school. Preliminary results are excellent. She has found that the age span of more than two years has not hindered the rapid progress of small groups of pupils working with remarkable independence.

Appleton educators are coming to grips with other problems. Superintendent of Schools J. P. Mann points out that "the development of our Continuous Progress Plan will have a marked effect on the educational program in the junior and senior high schools."

Under Continuous Progress gifted intermediate students begin junior high school work before completing their sixth year of elementary school. This has influenced junior high schools to adjust their programs to avoid wasting time in repetition. Visitors to Appleton point out that if Continuous Progress is desirable for the elementary school, a comparable philosophy may be equally useful for junior and senior high school.

A healthy atmosphere for experimentation exists in Appleton and the next few years are likely to see exciting developments in its schools.

Superintendent Mann says that the driving force behind Continuous Progress has been the city's director of elementary education, Martha Sorensen. Her graduate work at Northwestern University concentrated on the individual differences of children, a subject to which she has devoted much of her educational career.

"The facts are," says Miss Sorensen, "that children differ in many ways. The school must accept, respect and provide for these differences. This simply means that educational machinery must be flexible, materials of instruction varied, the means for learning many and the practices in tune with what we know about how children grow and develop."

Miss Sorensen first stimulated the community's interest with a study of its failures under the graded system and in 1947 other teachers joined her in considering organizational and reporting plans that would be based on the differences rather than the similarities of children.

By 1951 parents and school board members, as well as teachers, were considering the new program. That September it was established on an experimental basis with first-year students in one school. The following year it was extended to the beginning primary students at all schools. In 1957–58 the program was adopted throughout the elementary schools. No additional costs have been involved.

In their valuable work *The Nongraded Elementary School* (Harcourt, Brace and Co., 1959) Professors John I. Goodlad and Robert H. Anderson describe The School We Could Have:

"The facts and theory that suggest the kind of elementary school we advocate are largely a product of the twentieth century. The circumstances that led to the elementary school which we would abolish were characteristic of the nineteenth century. We believe that research on human development, learning, and curriculum, now available to educators, points to a nongraded type of elementary school organization."

Appleton appears to have made a good start.

> For further information about Continuous Progress contact:
>
> > J. P. Mann, Superintendent
> > Appleton Public Schools
> > 120 East Harris St.
> > Appleton, Wis.
>
> For related experimental programs see Appendix, pp. 176–78.

3. The Search for Hidden Talent:

NEW YORK CITY'S DEMONSTRATION GUIDANCE PROJECT

In recent years we have realized more sharply than ever that national survival may depend upon our utilization of all the talent within the United States.

For all our pride in democracy we have failed to tap the talents that lie dormant in many underprivileged groups—the largest and most significant being our Negro citizens. Dawning on many educators is the realization that equality of opportunity is not enough. Depressed slum-dwellers of all races, migratory workers or new arrivals from Puerto Rico may require special programs to make them aware that the opportunities do exist.

There is mounting indignation about juvenile delinquency in New York City. Surely there is also adult delinquency in the public apathy which permits the slum conditions of New York's Harlem.

From the heart of this area has emerged a powerful program which may present a blueprint for locating hidden talent and reducing delinquency —delinquency of the public as well as of the juveniles.

A BOY WHOM WE WILL CALL MANUEL is 17 years old. Born in Puerto Rico, he arrived in New York with his parents, his brother and sister during the tidal wave of immigration which brought more than 600,000 of his countrymen to the city.

Manuel lives in a dismal tenement crowded with relatives. His father no longer lives with the family and rarely contacts them. His mother has a low-salaried job. She can speak a little English but everyone speaks Spanish in the apartment. There is a television set but there are no books or English-language newspapers. There is no privacy.

The family life of his relatives unfolds before him. He sees and hears them as they love and as they squabble. Crowded conditions and life on the edge of poverty increase their tensions. Nothing is hidden.

For all that, Manuel is not a member of a gang. He has no weapons. He has never been in trouble with the police. He is a junior at George Washington High School. Contrary to the journalistic stereotype it is not a "blackboard jungle." Its 4,700 students, 40 percent of whom are Negroes or Puerto Ricans, respect the handsome colonial building and its 40-year tradition.

Last year Manuel passed every course. In spite of his environment he has achieved self-respect and he is liked by his classmates, whatever their color or family background. There is a good possibility that he will attend college.

Manuel is an example of the hidden talent uncovered by New York City's Demonstration Guidance Project. Its results have implications for all the underprivileged areas of the United States.

Launched in 1956 by the Board of Education's Commission on Integration, the project had as its objective "the early identification and stimulation of able students from low status socioeconomic homes."

It has been established that economically and socially privileged children score higher on intelligence tests than equally capable youngsters from culturally deprived homes. Conventional tests of mental ability are based on a pupil's facility with language and familiarity with U.S. culture patterns. Most recently arrived Puerto Ricans are doomed automatically to low scores regardless of their actual potential. To a lesser but considerable extent this applies to Negroes who have moved from the South, and to whites from comparably underprivileged backgrounds.

The Demonstration Guidance Project sought to discover the abilities lying dormant beneath environmental poverty, to raise the students' and parents' aspirations and stimulate the most capable to seek higher education. In most cases the targets of this project were youngsters who normally would have quit high school at the age of 16 to seek employment. If successful the project would accomplish a vital mission—increase the Nation's pool of skilled manpower.

The project focused on two schools, Junior High School 43 and George Washington High School which enrolls most of its graduates.

Junior High School 43 is located at 129th Street and Amsterdam Avenue. With rare exceptions its students are from low-income families living in crowded, substandard housing. Only a small percentage live in the new low-cost apartments which tower above the tenements.

When the Demonstration Guidance Project began in 1956, a survey revealed that 48 percent of the school's 1,400 students were Negro, 38 percent were of Puerto Rican background, 2 percent of other Spanish-speaking origin, 11 percent were white and 1 percent were Orientals.

About one-third of the students' parents had been born in Puerto Rico, another third had migrated from the deep South. Of tragic consequence was the added fact that only half the children lived with both father and mother.

This environment had wreaked massive damage. Less than half of Forty-Three's graduates went on to complete high school. Fewer than 10 percent of the junior high school graduates continued their education beyond high school. This contrasts with the estimated 50 percent of U.S. high school graduates who receive some form of higher education.

There were other grim facts. The Junior High School 43 students attending George Washington High School presented disciplinary problems in disproportion to their numbers. They lagged far behind classmates from other neighborhoods in reading and arithmetic.

Today these figures have been reversed. A new picture of the potential of depressed populations has emerged from the experiment.

The dropout rate of project students attending George Washington High School has been cut in half. It is less than the rate for the school as a whole. The percentage of these graduates eligible for college has leaped from about 9 percent to 36 percent. IQ scores of the project youngsters have risen sharply. In an era of sensational journalism during which residents of the area have been charged with crimes of the most extreme brutality, discipline problems at school have virtually disappeared.

How did it happen?

When the Board of Education gave Junior High School 43 the go-ahead, Principal Dan Schreiber and Guidance Counselor Ethel Flanagan mobilized their forces for the attack on apathy. Three full-time counselors were hired reducing the ratio to 375 students per counselor in contrast to New York City's usual 2,000 to 1 ratio. A psychologist and social worker joined the staff part-time and two full-time remedial mathematics teachers were added to the remedial reading teachers already employed. Another teacher was recruited to supervise a large-scale cultural enrichment program.

Then the entire student body was tested. An intelligence test prepared by Science Research Associates, relying on pictures rather than words, sought to overcome the students' verbal handicaps. The results were encouraging. Slightly more than half the students scored 100 or more, a notable improvement over their conventional IQ scores. This, in combination with the verbal IQ and Stanford achievement tests in reading and arithmetic, past records and teacher evaluations furnished a profile of each student. Counselors combed these records to select the largest number of experimental students to be included in the project.

Anyone who showed remote potential for college was to be chosen. Seven hundred seventeen seventh, eighth and ninth graders, more than half the student body, were finally selected.

By traditional U.S. standards this was an unorthodox group of high potential students. Three hundred twenty-nine were retarded 1.3 years or more in reading; 341 lagged by 1.3 years or more in mathematics.

Disregarding these formidable odds a massive assault was launched simultaneously on all fronts to lift the level of the experimental 717.

Two remedial reading teachers met groups of six students for four periods a week. In addition the reading experts initiated a training program for teachers of language arts, social studies, mathematics and science. One day each month these teachers attended inservice training classes during unassigned periods. They were treated as pupils and during each session they learned a basic reading skill.

When they returned to their classes they spread the gospel by devoting 10 minutes of each period for 2 weeks to the development of that skill as it related to their own subject matter. In this manner a new basic reading skill was handed down to all classes every month. This supplemented the reading lessons for small groups of students which met four times each week.

Twenty-eight teachers enrolled in a speech improvement course and led another attack on an acute student problem. This paid immediate dividends among youngsters struggling to replace Spanish inflections with the New York version of the English language.

Seven months after the beginning of the Demonstration

Guidance Project the effects of these programs were measured. Tests revealed that students receiving remedial reading assistance had registered a gain of 1.4 years in reading during the seven-month period. In one year *all* students gained more than a year and a half.

In mathematics the same procedure was followed. Two remedial mathematics teachers working with groups of six students four times a week also registered substantial gains.

Inseparably linked to this academic spurt was a guidance program which gave the students of Junior High School 43 a new look at themselves, their families and their career opportunities.

Each grade had its own counselor who met youngsters in individual sessions and in weekly group meetings. Concentrating on careers and career planning, the counselors shattered the students' belief that they were limited automatically by the occupations of their parents, by color and by the boundaries of neighborhood.

One of the counselors, Mrs. Susan Blakey, developed an effective technique to stimulate ambition. On charts listing requirements for professions and skilled occupations, she placed pictures of Negroes and Puerto Ricans as well as whites who had distinguished themselves in these fields. When a child indicated that a parent had discouraged him from pursuing a career because of color Mrs. Blakey, herself a Negro, would pack up her chart and visit the youngster's home.

In the beginning parents were somewhat loath to meet the counselors. For every 10 interviews requested by counselors during the first year there was only 1 proposed by a parent. Two years later 10 parents would request meetings for every 1 summoned by a counselor.

If parents could not meet counselors during working hours the appointments would be scheduled early in the morning or at night. One counselor had meetings with parents on 14 successive Sundays.

During the first year of the project counselors conducted over 2,000 individual interviews with the experimental students in addition to the weekly group guidance sessions. During this period there were over 800 contacts with parents.

The cultural enrichment program worked hand-in-hand with guidance. Many students of Forty-Three had never seen the world beyond their own drab, crowded streets. Suddenly that world was opened to them.

They visited art galleries, saw Broadway plays, heard symphony orchestras, were welcomed by great universities, attended performances at the Metropolitan Opera, were exposed to college spirit at football games and during campus visits.

And how did these youngsters from culturally barren homes respond?

Of a painting at the Museum of Modern Art: "When I looked at it, it made me feel warm and wonderful. It sort of picked me up and made me feel glad that I was living."

A symphony brought these comments: "I was very excited to hear a real symphony orchestra play for me . . . I thought it was going to be corny but it turned out to be fun . . . I don't think it's fair for a person to call someone a 'square' just because they like classical music . . . some of us didn't realize how much we liked this kind of music because we don't hear it often. I think he [the conductor] is a very nice and friendly and learned man."

Reporting on visits to Carnegie Hall one youngster

wrote: "I like rock-n-roll but went to all [concerts]. Once I took my six-year-old cousin to Carnegie Hall with the school group. I had to watch her. She nudged me during the performance and said, 'Pretty, isn't it.' I have become interested in operas. I never went to an opera before, but now I will continue to go. Now, my parents, who have never gone to opera or concerts, have made plans to go."

In 1958, Junior High School 43 purchased 100 subscriptions to concerts of the New York Philharmonic, the largest number of tickets bought by a single school in the history of the orchestra. Although students who wished to attend could get free tickets by applying privately to their teachers, many paid a substantial share of the price.

This enrichment program was integrated with curriculum. One hundred seventh grade social studies students visited the Roosevelt Library and home at Hyde Park. For many it was the first trip outside the city. Ninth grade social studies classes attended the World Trade Fair at the New York Coliseum.

Top students interested in science and engineering toured the Sloan-Kettering Institute for Cancer Research and atomic energy facilities at the Brookhaven National Laboratory. Youngsters who had once felt unwelcome anywhere but in the back alleys of Harlem stood alongside engineering students in a Manhattan College laboratory and carried out experiments successfully.

Before each trip parents received a letter from Principal Schreiber explaining its purpose, outlining the preparatory work at school and the intended followup.

The cultural program within the school itself was expanded.

Films of 14 classics of English literature were rented

and made available to all classes. Representatives of 10 foreign consulates presented songs, dances and travelogs at ninth grade assemblies. Capacity audiences watched professional theater groups perform in the school auditorium.

As the program unfolded and new horizons opened to the boys and girls of 129th Street, guidance counselors began to feel the full impact of their youngsters' problems.

There was a 12-year-old girl who cooked, cleaned, washed and ironed for her family and cared for three younger brothers and sisters. Tests revealed her as a student of high potential but worn out from her labors at home she was unable to do homework, barely stayed awake during class, failed in some courses. Guidance counselors described her capabilities to her working mother and helped to make arrangements lightening the child's burdens at home. Her scholastic average soared into the eighties.

Some problems seemed insurmountable. One father hurled his ambitious son's books out of the window when the boy brought them home for study. Junior High School 43 kept one classroom open after school so this youngster and others without privacy at home could work quietly.

Counselors made arrangements with parents in crowded apartments to turn television sets off between certain hours so students could complete homework and hammered out agreements with younger brothers and sisters to permit budding scholars to work without interruption.

The parents of these children were, for the most part, people of limited education struggling for survival in a strange environment. Yet with few exceptions they cooperated fully in the drive to lift the level of their children's aspirations.

In May 1957, eight months after the project began, 66.3 percent of the parents returned a questionnaire asking for their opinion of its effectiveness. Of these, 59.2 percent said it had helped their children but only 38.7 percent expressed an interest in seeing their youngster's counselor.

One year later the survey was repeated. This time 70.6 percent replied. Now 82.6 percent of the respondents said the project had helped their children and 84 percent were now interested in talking to the counselor.

This willingness to work with the school was reflected by attendance at parent meetings. Throughout New York City only 10 percent of junior high school parents attend daytime meetings but 23 percent of Forty-Three's parents met throughout the year to learn how they could contribute to the project's success.

The intellectual ferment at Forty-Three showed up in many ways. For one thing there was a 300 percent increase in the use of library books. In a "Readers Are Leaders" program, 118 students received buttons for completing at least 6 recommended books, 49 read at least 12. Pupils *purchased* more than 1,000 volumes through a school discount plan and each buyer received a personalized book plate to encourage the building of a personal library. An additional 800 volumes were sold at the annual Book Fair.

During the summer before the first experimental group moved up to George Washington High School, 36 students attended special classes in reading. In six weeks they gained seven months in average growth.

But the great test was still ahead. The high school had a proud tradition of scholarship and its Principal, Henry T. Hillson, did not intend to jeopardize its reputation. Hillson, a six-foot, five-and-a-half inch graduate of Dartmouth, was determined to give project students every possible opportunity but they were to make their way on achievement rather than sympathy. He was all for the cultural enrichment program but he believed that a solid academic groundwork was the essential prerequisite for college.

In September 1957, he looked at the records of the 148 experimental pupils from Forty-Three who had entered his school and he wondered if they could survive.

They had come a long way in that year at Forty-Three but they still had far to go. Eighty-nine percent were still below grade level in reading; 88 percent lagged in arithmetic. Tests revealed that they trailed their classmates from other neighborhoods in social studies background, correctness in writing, general vocabulary and quantitative thinking.

"Utterly ridiculous!" said some of the George Washington teachers, contemplating the newcomers. "They can't read, they can't write and they can't spell!"

Could one expect them to succeed in such a short time? They had been in the project only from September to June and now were to be thrust into high school. Perhaps future graduates of Forty-Three, bolstered by one and two extra years of the project, would make the grade but could one really expect success from the group entering in September 1957?

Having considered every reason why the experiment might fail Hillson hurled all the resources of his school into its success.

Project pupils were given double periods in English to narrow the greatest gap between themselves and more fortunate classmates.

Project classes were kept small. In mathematics and languages they were limited to 10–15 students. Students who showed potential but needed extra help were tutored in groups of three and four.

A psychiatric social worker and psychologist joined a team of guidance counselors intensifying the program begun at the junior high school. Weekly group guidance sessions focused on high school life, on college and on future occupations.

Results were so dramatic that they amazed even the counselors. One boy, of obvious high intelligence, concealed a desperate home situation by rebelliousness and erratic classwork. The joint efforts of teachers and counselors channeled the boy's energies into creative writing. One of his works has been selected for a national anthology, he has a better understanding of his home situation and his behavior has improved. In addition to passing all subjects he completed two advanced courses during the summer.

Trips to colleges continued to unlock hidden talents and unexpected enthusiasms. The dean of admissions of Amherst College invited high-ranking project boys to the college for a weekend. One of the boys, though a gifted student, had been withdrawn and uncommunicative. At Amherst, welcomed by students and faculty, shown about the lovely grounds, introduced to a wonderful world suddenly within reach, the boy began to talk freely. He still does!

In the 1958–59 term, project students at George Washington attended eight Broadway plays, the New York City Ballet, eight Philharmonic concerts and the Metropolitan Museum of Art. They toured the United States Military Academy and the Brookhaven National Laboratory. Per-

haps the highlight of the year was the visit of 198 students
to a performance of "A Midsummer Night's Dream" at the
American Shakespeare Festival in Stratford, Conn.

The intensity of the counseling program had far-
reaching effects. More than two-thirds of the students were
interviewed 4 times or more during the first year, some as
many as 20 times. Counselors acted as liaison between students and teachers. The teachers, fortified by information
about the youngsters and their families were better
equipped to handle problems arising in class.

One boy, the youngest of 14 children, was inarticulate,
withdrawn, forgotten at home. Buoyed by the counselors'
interest in their son, proud of his newly discovered abilities, parental attitudes were changed. The boy ended the
year with an 89 percent average and a brighter outlook on
life.

At the end of the year, Principal Hillson added up the
results. Of the 148 experimental pupils who had entered
his school, 133 remained.

The number of students passing all academic courses
was five times greater than among the group sent by Forty-
Three the year before the project began. Eighteen project
students averaged over 80 percent in all courses. Fourteen
averaged 85 percent or over in English; 10 in mathematics;
14 in science and 23 in foreign languages. There was
nothing comparable in the records of the earlier group.

Discipline problems of a serious nature had ended, a re-
versal of past history when graduates of Forty-Three had
caused a disproportionate amount of trouble at George
Washington.

A study of the social acceptance of project students at
the high school conducted by the Board of Education's

Bureau of Educational Research concluded that "after one year in high school, pupils involved in the Demonstration Guidance Project received general acceptance from other project students and from nonproject students. In no class were the project pupils, as a group, rejected."

The report went on to state that the pupils' images of themselves were no different than the self-images of the other youngsters.

As had been expected the project classes which entered George Washington in 1958 and 1959 are exceeding the performance of the original group. Even so, as many as 40 members of the original group may be eligible for college entrance in September 1960.

In May 1959, 105 project students took an advanced form of the same verbal IQ test they had taken in February 1956 (Pintner Test of General Ability). To those who cling to the belief that mental ability scores are unchanging the results are a revelation. Seventy-eight pupils showed an increase, 64 gaining more than 5 points; 25 showed a drop, 2 were identical.

Gains in reading ability were equally dramatic. When the project began, the experimental students lagged about 1½ years behind the national norm.

In 2½ years they had gained a full four years in reading growth bringing them up to the national level.

Dropouts were cut in half.

As the senior class at George Washington approaches graduation its leadership includes several project students. Among contenders for top scholastic honors are three boys with averages of 95.3 percent, 94.7 percent and 93.4 percent.

An exhibit prepared by two of these youngsters won

third prize in the New York City Science Fair. One of the winners, a shy boy who had not expected to go to college, was invited to participate in Columbia University's Science Honors Program. Other project students take part in athletics, social committees and help to staff the school newspaper.

"The most dramatic fact about this project," says Henry Hillson, the realist who insisted on academic performance, "is that we can salvage a great number of boys and girls who would otherwise be lost. Many of these youngsters will not be able to attend college but if we make it possible for them to finish high school successfully they'll be on the way to becoming self-respecting citizens and assets to this community."

The Demonstration Guidance Project cost $71,000 during its first year at Junior High School 43, $119,500 the year it was extended to George Washington. The Board of Education paid all costs except for $10,000 a year donated by the College Entrance Examination Board and $11,000 a year contributed by the National Scholarship Service and Fund for Negro Students.

The latter group played a prominent role in launching the experiment. Its president, Richard L. Plaut, had been a sparkplug of his organization's "Southern Project." This search for hidden talent had helped hundreds of Negro youngsters to move from segregated high schools in the South to nonsegregated colleges and universities throughout the United States. Their academic achievements reaffirmed the knowledge that inadequate education stems from social and economic factors rather than racial or ethnic characteristics.

Plaut headed the Guidance Subcommission of the Board

of Education's Commission on Integration which proposed the Junior High School 43 program. The board's Bureau of Educational and Vocational Guidance then developed the project and its Bureau of Education Research added its resources.

They drew on the wisdom and warmth of Dan Schreiber, the principal of 43, who in 15 years of Harlem teaching had never lost faith in the power of education and the potential of all people.

A gray-haired man with deep-set brown eyes which mirror his convictions, Schreiber says, "No ethnic group has a corner on all the brains or all the ignorance. People are essentially the same. Given the same breaks the Puerto Rican or Negro youngster has as much chance of winning a Nobel Prize as the white child. We need all the talent we can get and we can't have a decent society if we deny opportunity to youngsters because of race or origin or economic condition. The whole American tradition is based on the rise of underprivileged groups. Once they were Italian or Irish or Jewish—now they're Puerto Rican or Negro."

Dan Schreiber is no longer principal of Junior High School 43. Recently he was named coordinator of the Board of Education's "Higher Horizons" program which will extend many of the lessons learned by the Demonstration Guidance Project to 31 elementary and 13 junior high schools. Financed by the board's initial appropriation of $500,000, it will seek to raise the aspirations of youngsters from the third grade onward. In the beginning it will be limited to third and seventh grade students. Broader-based than the pilot project it is not so much concerned with preparation for college as with preparation for life.

New York is not the only city facing the problem of depressed people in squalid slums. Visitors from Chicago, Philadelphia, Cincinnati, Baltimore, Washington, D.C., Indianapolis and other cities have watched the Demonstration Guidance Project in action and considered whether more teachers and guidance counselors might not be preferable to more policemen.

Now, like Dan Schreiber, they look forward to higher horizons.

For further information about the Demonstration Guidance Project or Higher Horizons contact:

> Daniel Schreiber, Coordinator
> Higher Horizons
> New York City Board of Education
> 110 Livingston St.
> Brooklyn 1, N.Y.

For further information about the role of George Washington High School contact:

> Henry Hillson, Principal
> George Washington High School
> 192d St., Audubon Ave.
> New York 40, N.Y.

4. Freeing the Teacher for Teaching:

THE TEACHER AIDES
OF BAY CITY, MICH.

Physicians, lawyers, engineers and architects utilize the services of secretaries and clerks to handle their paperwork and nonprofessional duties. Teachers, overburdened by the number of their pupils and the magnitude of their responsibilities, are required to waste precious hours in nonprofessional activities.

A commonsense answer to this problem has been developed at Bay City, Mich. and has spread to other parts of the United States. It has immediate application in most schools for it is designed to free the teacher for teaching.

THE MOMENT YOU STEP INTO THE FIRST
grade room of the Thomas Jefferson Elementary School in
Bay City, Mich., you realize that you are in the presence
of a superior teacher. It is evident in the sparkle of the
children's eyes, in the atmosphere of cheerful self-discipline and in the physical attractiveness of the room.

The teacher is Virginia Patrick. She is the mother of a
20-year-old daughter and 12-year-old son. She completed
requirements for teacher certification during the summer
of 1959 at the age of 40.

"Virginia is vivacious and alert," says her principal.
"This is her first year of teaching but she handles herself
like a veteran."

Virginia Patrick's new career is one of many unexpected
by-products of the teacher aide experiment. This was inaugurated in the Bay City schools to relieve teachers of
time-consuming, nonprofessional chores. Virginia was one
of eight aides selected to pioneer the program in 1953.

As of November 1, 1959, 42 Michigan school systems
were utilizing aides in elementary, junior and senior high
schools. Throughout the United States, communities have

adopted variations of the Bay City plan. It is applicable wherever overcrowding exists because of a shortage of classrooms or teachers. Beyond that the increased use of aides to relieve teachers of paperwork has proved useful even where classes are of manageable size.

The Bay City program originated with Charles B. Park, a genial, energetic man who became superintendent of schools in 1948. Casting about for a way out of the dilemma of having too few teachers and too few classrooms to handle his growing school enrollment, he decided there was only one immediate solution: to make more effective use of the training and skills of teachers already on his staff.

That sounded fine, but how could it be done? The answer worked out by Park and his associates with the help of Central Michigan University was wonderfully simple: just as hospitals brought in nurses' aides during World War II to relieve overworked nurses, Bay City would bring nonprofessional local people into the schools as teacher aides to take over the overburdened teachers' routine work.

Simple as the basic idea was, Park went about putting it into effect scientifically, a step at a time. First, he wanted to find out just how much time teachers actually were spending on nonprofessional duties, so he organized a stopwatch survey of each of the 137 teachers then in the Bay City elementary schools. Each teacher's every move was timed precisely throughout the day. The findings were, to say the least, provocative.

They showed that a teacher's priceless gift—the ability to teach—was being squandered on routine chores: watering plants, cleaning blackboards, monitoring lunchrooms, policing playgrounds, putting on children's leggings, filling out elaborate attendance sheets, collecting class funds for dozens of causes.

The minute spent here, the minute lost there, snowballed into totals ranging from one hour and a quarter to four hours and nine minutes of each teacher's teaching day. The overall average: 26 percent of a teacher's time (not counting nearly 12 hours a week of overtime work outside the classroom) was devoted to nonteaching chores.

These findings convinced Park that teacher aides could make a useful contribution to education in Bay City. He set about recruiting them from the talent which exists in any American community—housewives and working women who love children, believe in education and want to do useful, interesting work. From among 64 volunteers, Park and his assistants selected 8.

One of them was Virginia Patrick. Happily married to Donald Patrick, part owner of a Bay City tavern, she loved the warmth and sensitivity of children. Since her own youngsters were at school all day, she missed their merriment and their problems. Like her husband, Virginia had completed two years of college before marriage, and since then she had taken courses in painting and ceramics.

Until she was recruited as a teacher aide, however, her artistic talents and way with youngsters were largely unused. But as aide to Betty Beetham, a skilled first grade teacher in Bay City's Dolsen School, Virginia's gifts enriched the education of 50 pupils. They also increased Betty's effectiveness as a teacher. She enabled Betty to give pupils the individual attention usually possible only in much smaller classes.

This is what an observer saw during a typical morning in Betty Beetham's humming first grade classroom:

8:00. Virginia arrives and Betty, a young, attractive woman with an infectious smile, outlines the day's work plan to her aide. Then Virginia distributes work materials at each table and takes her place at the aide's desk in the rear of the room.

8:30. The class begins. After the teacher leads the Pledge of Allegiance, Virginia begins checking attendance. The name, address and previous number of days missed must be entered for each absentee and brought to the principal's office by 9:30. Before having an aide, Betty wasted many minutes checking the 50 names.

With Virginia taking over the clerical chores, Betty begins immediately with the first item on her first grade work program: "show and tell." During this brief period youngsters describe their latest experiences and parade their new acquisitions.

Ronny, pirouetting like a fashion model, exhibits his bright red sweater. Then a boy in blue jeans points to a picture hanging on the wall. "I had a puppy like Tip in that picture," he says, "but he died."

After a brief discussion of the death of pets, a chubby girl rises and announces dolefully, "My mommy's going to have a baby."

The class oohs and ahs, this momentous news wiping out memory of the puppy's death.

As Betty continues the "show and tell," a small procession of youngsters troops to her aide's desk. A boy slouches in late and mumbles his explanation ("I was afraid it might rain and I'd get my new jacket wet"). Several children turn in their weekly milk money and Virginia oversees a mounting pile of coins. She has become an expert bookkeeper. Among other things she handles funds for Christmas and Easter seals, cancer and heart drives, Junior Red Cross and an annual magic show.

8:45. Betty Beetham has divided the class into four groups of about 13 pupils each, according to reading proficiency. She presents new material to one group of children while Virginia takes another to a corner of the room for a drill on yesterday's vocabulary. An aide never presents new work and is restricted largely to conducting drills and reviews at the teacher's direction.

8:50. Virginia conducts a flashcard drill for the slower learners. A tousle-haired boy with piercing black eyes sits at her feet. He leans intently toward the cards as if to devour them. He is a repeater in the first grade and the extra attention Virginia has given him is reflected by his dawning understanding of the words flashing before him. He can barely restrain his desire to shout them during someone else's turn. Finally Virginia holds a card toward him and a big grin spreads across his face.

"What word is this?" Virginia asks.

"'Funny,'" he replies quickly, "that word is 'funny'."

"And it begins with —?"

"With an 'F'," he says, glancing triumphantly at his schoolmates, "'funny' begins with an 'F'."

Before Betty Beetham had an aide she could not devote sufficient time to the slow learners without handicapping the progress of the rest of the class. But Virginia's hours with the tousle-haired boy and others have had unmistakeable results. Soon some of them will be promoted to advanced groups.

9:10. Six-year-old Thelma falls from her chair and sprawls on the floor, her papers flying in every direction. Betty smiles at her reassuringly but continues teaching the new work. Virginia leaves her review group to help Thelma collect her papers and herself. Then she hugs her, settles her back to work and returns to the review group.

9:20. The music and physical education period begins. Without her aide Betty would have to play the piano while supervising 50 singing, dancing, running, jumping children. Since Virginia is also a pianist, Betty can now participate with her class. She dances a minuet with them. The class is aware that their teacher is among them, offering assistance and laughing with them.

9:50. Virginia obtains the class milk and supervises its distribution. While it is being sipped, Betty describes a new class project. A 10-minute quiet period follows. Fifty small heads rest on their desks.

During an endless morning Virginia performed an endless list of chores. She put up wall decorations, handled messages from the principal's office, dusted the room, wrote on the blackboard, fetched books from the library and handled a score of clerical details. But beyond the performance of such routine duties she also contributed her special gifts to the class. The first graders of Dolsen School created delightful animal sculpture because of Virginia's knowledge of ceramics.

Betty Beetham summed up her aide's contribution very simply: "With Virginia helping me I can teach a large class for a full day without depriving the children of individual attention."

Other Bay City teachers confirmed Betty's statement.

"I never thought it possible," an older teacher admitted, "that I would enjoy the presence of another adult in my class. I expected that my aide would make me nervous, that I would be inhibited in front of the children. Instead

I find that my aide's appreciation of my skill as a teacher is very satisfying. She doesn't hinder my teaching; she stimulates it."

Marian Oberg, a teacher who had an aide the first year of the experiment and taught without one later, described the difference in her own effectiveness: "With an aide, after presenting new material I could assign a written exercise on the work and correct papers immediately. I could discuss errors on the same day while the lesson was fresh in the children's minds. I had the time because my aide handled all the interruptions that would have prevented me from correcting papers in class. Teaching 42 children without an aide has left me swamped. I can't pay enough attention to the slow learners without handicapping the rest of the class, and I can't spend time correcting papers right after new lessons. I have to take them home with me. When I bring them in next day the children have more difficulty understanding their mistakes."

Bay City, a community of 55,000 located at the mouth of the Saginaw River 100 miles northwest of Detroit, was once the lumber queen of the world. It now boasts 100 diversified industries, ranging from potato chips to shipbuilding. But nothing in its history would suggest diversification in education. The teacher aide program began in Bay City because of imaginative Charles Park and the unorthodox faculty of Central Michigan University in Mount Pleasant, 45 miles away.

Park, who has been a teacher and school superintendent for 28 of his 57 years, was once the Mount Pleasant superintendent of schools and doubled as associate director of teacher training at the college. For nine years he had lived in Central Michigan's educational ferment and his closest friends were responsible for the excitement. One was the university's president, Dr. Charles L. Anspach, a former Chevrolet executive. The other was Vice President Woodward C. Smith, director of its Division of Public Services, which spreads the gospel of education in 38 Michigan counties with the fervor of an agriculture extension service.

"Someone," Park recalls, "has described a university as a lot of old buildings set back from the street with vines crawling on the outside and professors crawling on the in. Well, Central Michigan is about as far from that as it's possible to get."

When Park was named superintendent of the Bay City schools in 1948, he brought from Central Michigan "a willingness to be a bit daring." He needed it. Fourteen of Bay City's 15 elementary schools were at least 40 years old. Almost every classroom overflowed. Park's first step was to draft a long-range building plan.

Spurred by the new superintendent's enthusiasm, townspeople launched a drive to increase taxes from $2 to $4 a thousand for a 15-year, pay-as-you-go school-building program. Amby Maxwell, manager of the local chamber of commerce, raised money among businessmen to pay for advertisements urging a vote for higher taxes. His sales talk was quite unorthodox.

"We need your money to make sure that this program wins at the polls," he said, "because if it does it will cost you *more* money."

Bay City voted overwhelmingly for the new schools. But the school-building solution was not enough for Park. He spent weekends fishing the Au Sable River with his cronies, Anspach and Smith. Between bites they discussed the double load being borne by Bay City teachers because of intense overcrowding and the growing number of nonprofessional duties. Gradually they evolved the teacher aide idea.

Park appealed to the Ford Foundation's Fund for the Advancement of Education for financial help in putting the plan over. In 1952 the fund approved a five-year grant, to be administered by Central Michigan's Division of Public Services. With Bay City's building program well under way, Park resigned as superintendent to direct the experiment from Central Michigan University.

The first step was the time study of the Bay City teachers' workdays. Next came the recruitment of the teacher aides. There were no advertisements. Park and his assistants spoke to PTA officers, prominent citizens and the dean of the local junior college. They described the type of people they sought and within a few days they had 64 names.

"We were bowled over by the quality of the people who were willing to help," says Park. "Only 1 of the 64 asked about salary." (It was to be $45 a week.) "I'd say we tapped less than 10 percent of the community in our search. The talents and skills that were available and unused were a revelation."

Park established several criteria for selecting aides so his study would not be weighted unfairly. No former teacher or trainee was to be considered. Those chosen were to be the kind of people available in any community and were to have at least a high school education.

Park and his staff conducted unannounced interviews in the candidates' homes, noting particularly their attitudes about children. "In some cases," Park says, "we chose high school graduates who were enthusiastic and person-

able in place of junior college graduates who had mil-
dewed."

The eight aides who were selected for the first experiment ranged in age from 19-year-old Kathleen Barber,
a former drugstore clerk, to Mrs. Dorothy Secor, a 42-
year-old grandmother. They included Mrs. Doris Hewitt,
mother of two, high school graduate and former instructor
for the telephone company; the talented Virginia Patrick,
and Jacquelyn Bedford, a department store salesgirl whose
training included choral singing and dramatics.

For all its apparent simplicity, the teacher aide idea had
to overcome some not-so-simple problems. There was, for
example, the psychological hurdle created by generations
of teaching within classroom privacy.

"I was dead set against the idea," a school principal re-
members. "I could see my teachers losing status while a
lot of untrained busybodies cluttered up their classrooms."

Park explained to faculty meetings that the aides were
to be entirely subordinate, that they would not be permitted to teach and that personality conflicts would be re-
solved by transferring the aide.

"What about the aides' salaries?" asked the economy ad-
vocates. "Why pay $45 a week to untrained people?"

Park reminded them that Bay City's budget for salaries
was based on a teacher for every 30 pupils, a ratio made
impossible by an inadequate supply of teachers and classrooms. Park estimated that a teacher with an aide could
handle 45 pupils, one and a half times as many as a teacher
alone. Since the aide's salary was half that of a teacher,
the total expenditure would remain the same.

Criticism of the experiment was not confined to Bay
City. A professor at the University of Michigan's School

of Education cited one of the hazards. "You can't divide a teacher's duties into so-called 'professional' and 'non-professional' categories. Why, the most routine task of a teacher may be of the greatest importance to a child. Even such a small matter as helping a youngster put on his coat and boots may help in cementing his relationship with the teacher. The really skilled teacher may pick up more clues to a child's needs during routine classroom chores than in the formal learning periods."

Some teacher organizations also were skeptical. Under improper direction, they warned, nonprofessionals in the classroom might endanger high teaching standards or be used to keep professional salaries depressed. They pointed out that a tightfisted board of education might concentrate on hiring aides rather than teachers, even if the latter were available, and wreak havoc with teacher recruiting.

Despite such misgivings, the teacher aide program was put into effect in September 1953. On the first day Virginia Patrick and her colleagues walked uneasily into class. In one room a youngster spotted his new teacher and her aide and muttered, "Oh, no! Not two of them!"

But thanks to a farsighted training program developed by Harriett Van Antwerp, Bay City's elementary school director, the aides made a speedy adjustment.

Once a week Miss Van Antwerp conducted a two-hour workshop for aides ranging over the whole school program. She was the first of many professionals to be startled by their ability.

"We had been haughty and high-hat," she says, "to think that only professional people could contribute to the schools. In more than 20 years of supervising I have never had a group that has had so many constructive ideas and is so eager for knowledge."

As the 1953–54 school year wore on, the teachers became increasingly enthusiastic about the program, and the aides received tangible evidence of the children's feelings.

When Doris Hewitt was confined to her home by illness, she received a bed jacket from her class. It was beautiful but somewhat oversized, and when she returned it to a local department store the salesman said, "So you're the lady who caused all the excitement. I never saw children so fussy about a purchase. They made me take out every bed jacket in the place before they chose this. Then they insisted upon seeing the gift box and the ribbon, and they wouldn't leave until I had the jacket pressed and wrapped. After all that they made me retie the bow."

Two days before Christmas, one of the aides reported that she would be unable to come to school because her own child was ill. The night before Christmas she was in the child's room when six youngsters from class came quietly to the front of her house and serenaded her softly with Christmas carols.

These were personal indications of affection, but by June 1954, Park and his colleagues were well along in their hard-boiled appraisal of the first year's experiment. They measured the achievement of the rooms with aides and compared them with rooms without aides. Omitting the kindergarten, they selected two comparison or "control" rooms without aides for each of the seven with an aide. One control room in each grade had as many pupils as the room with an aide; the other control room had about 30 pupils per teacher. Students and teachers in control and aide rooms were matched as closely as possible, the students having taken intelligence tests in advance. The achievement tests covered a 7-month period. They showed that children in rooms with aides made above-average progress: the pupils were at the stage normally reached only after 7.3 months. The children in rooms with a teacher only were found to be at the 6.4-month stage. Five of the experimental rooms containing 45 or more pupils showed greater progress than the seven control rooms with only 30 students.

Then new stopwatch studies of teachers with aides were made. When compared with the original time studies that began the experiment, they showed that a teacher with an aide:

* Spent one-fifth more time making assignments.

* Added more than a full hour of classroom recitation each day.

* Gave 27 percent more individual help to each pupil; when the aide's own contribution was considered, each pupil was found to have received 90 percent more individual help than previously.

* Spent 48 percent less time on nonprofessional and clerical chores.

* Gave more personal counseling to students.

* Spent over twice as much time on important lesson plans.

This was encouraging, but Park and company were still not convinced. They conducted opinion polls of aides, pupils, parents and teachers.

One of every five parents with children in aide classes was questioned. There was 100 percent agreement among them that their youngsters had enjoyed school more in 1953–54 than in other years. Eighty-three percent felt that their children had learned more than in previous years. All said they preferred that their children have aides in the future.

Ninety-four percent of the pupils polled—all sixth graders—said they liked having an aide, 84 percent believed they had learned more and 94 percent said their teacher had been able to help them more.

From the start most Bay City teachers had been enthusiastic about the program. By the end of the trial year the remaining teachers and principals, almost without exception, also had become boosters.

Something else important happened, too. Virginia Patrick, stimulated by her happy experiences as an aide, decided to become a full-fledged teacher. With two years of college behind her, she drove 40 miles to Standish, Mich., two nights a week for extension courses offered by Central Michigan University. Her husband joined her to complete his own college career.

Today, Virginia Patrick is one of four former Bay City aides who have either become full-fledged teachers or are completing certification requirements. Two of the original eight are still acting as aides. One, Marie Schmidt, is in her seventh year with the same kindergarten teacher, Mrs. Marian Schur.

There are 46 children in Mrs. Schur's class at Woodside School. Speaking of her aide, Mrs. Schur says, "The biggest contribution she makes is that she gives me more time to plan with and for the children. I am a better teacher in this state of emergency. Teaching a class of this size would be drudgery if not an impossibility without the help of an aide."

Mrs. Schur's is only one of five large classes at Woodside School assisted by aides. At least one of the teachers, Mrs. June Bailey, is frank to admit that she opposed the idea in the beginning.

"I was one of those who did not want an aide," she recalls, "because I consider myself an independent type of person. I have a class of 47 this year and I've changed my mind. I'm very well pleased with my aide. She takes over all my paperwork and gives me time for the important things in teaching."

The hue and cry against teacher aides has subsided. So have the delegations sent to Bay City with preconceived opinions. Teacher organizations are beginning to realize that aides, far from undermining teachers, enable them to function more professionally.

Although the Fund for the Advancement of Education grant has expired, the teacher aide idea has spread from the elementary schools of Bay City to Michigan junior and senior high schools. The State Board of Education now certifies aides who meet the standards established by Central Michigan University.

They range from the retired metals and machine shop expert who assists at Mount Morris High School to the woman in the one-room Connell School in Ottawa County. The expanded use of aides in handling clerical work for teaching teams in Michigan and other States presages their future utilization.

Charles Park, who started it all, is now director of special studies for Central Michigan University. It is not surprising that he and his colleagues have inaugurated new programs in teacher recruitment, education and utilization. They still have that "willingness to be a bit daring."

For further information about teacher aides contact:

> Charles B. Park
> Director of Special Studies
> Central Michigan University
> Mount Pleasant, Mich.

For related experimental programs see Appendix, pp. 178–79.

5. Television Pioneer:

WASHINGTON COUNTY, MD.

Many teachers and teacher's organizations have reacted with fear to the specter of television in the classroom. Today we accept the fact that the printing press has helped to liberate man from ignorance. Tomorrow we may regard the fusion of picture and sound with equal respect.

At a time when there are not enough competent teachers for our children, television offers the possibility of spreading their rare gifts to greater numbers of students than ever before possible. Television has the power to bring the world into the classroom.

As utilized in Washington County, Md., television does not supplant the teacher. It enlarges him.

ONE OF THE MOST ACTIVE TELEVISION networks in the world is centered in Hagerstown, Md. More than one hundred "live" programs each week are transmitted from 5 studios to 37 elementary and secondary schools containing 16,500 of the 18,000 students of Washington County.

The most extensive experiment of its type, its implications are far-reaching, its ultimate impact on U.S. education incalculable. Although only in the fourth year of a five-year trial run, educational television has proved itself in Washington County, a tranquil community of 85,000 lying in the fertile Cumberland Valley. The experience of these schools in guiding TV through its birth and infancy can be of invaluable help to other communities.

The adoption of closed-circuit television occurred eight long years after Washington County school administrators and teachers began to re-examine and revise curriculum. Television was tailored to fit educational needs; education was not molded to television.

A happy blending of equipment from the Radio-Electronics-Television Manufacturers Association, funds from the Ford Foundation's Fund for the Advancement of Education, and coaxial cable from the Chesapeake and Potomac Telephone Co. brought television physically to Washington County. Philosophically it arrived through the cooperative efforts of hundreds of teachers, parents and school officials.

"Our use of television," says Superintendent of Schools William M. Brish, "emphasizes the creativeness of teaching. We find that television, as one resource of education, motivates the interest of pupils and is an intense inservice aid to classroom teachers."

How does it work? Mrs. Pearl C. Snively teaches seventh grade core classes. Core combines social studies and language arts and is the heart of the seventh grade curriculum. It relates the history and way of life of people to the geography of their lands. This is how Mrs. Snively televised a recent lesson.

At 9:05 a.m. Mrs. Snively stood under the lights of studio B, one of five studios operated by the board of education adjacent to its headquarters in Hagerstown. Launching a new unit in the core program, her assignment was to present a 40-minute Overview of the Middle East. Her telecast would reach 1,950 seventh graders in eight schools. Two cameras faced her and the battery of visual aids she had assembled. In the control room the director, linked to his crew by telephone headset, reviewed the script written by the teacher.

In preparing her lesson Mrs. Snively had unique advantages denied the typical classroom teacher. With a teaching schedule limited to one telecast per day, freed from the clerical chores, grading of examinations and miscellaneous activities that crowd the conventional teaching day,

Mrs. Snively had concentrated on preparing her lesson. For more than 10 hours she had worked out her presentation, utilizing resources not available in most junior high schools. A library of books, photographs and films was at her disposal. She had communicated with the embassies of the countries involved, had sought out local residents with firsthand knowledge of the area, had borrowed materials from industry and an art museum.

One month earlier, teachers in the classrooms scheduled to receive the telecast had received detailed guide-sheets in which Mrs. Snively had outlined the scope of the lesson. Included were suggestions for the teachers' followthrough during a subsequent 55-minute period. These were based on the seventh grade core curriculum which had been developed at summer and winter workshops by both studio and classroom teachers.

But Mrs. Snively's presentation reflected more than good organization and the utilization of new resources. It displayed the talents of a gifted teacher with a rich educational background. Her lesson fused her graduate work in literature at Johns Hopkins University, musical training at the Peabody Conservatory and intimate knowledge of subject matter gained in postgraduate courses at the University of Maryland.

The lesson began with an excerpt from a recording of the "Arabian Dance" from Tchaikovsky's *Nutcracker Suite* played against a closeup of a clearly defined map of the area. Then Mrs. Snively took over. First she discussed the continents of the Eastern Hemisphere and as she named and described them the cameras superimposed them vividly on a large globe. In the classrooms one television receiver provided for each 20 students enabled everyone to see and hear clearly.

As Mrs. Snively narrowed the focus of the lesson to the lands of the Middle East, she said, "Now we'll have an opportunity to learn what gifts have come to us today from those nations that most directly affect the way we live in the Western Hemisphere. We might have some questions to think about such as these" . . .

As she enumerated each question it appeared on the screen in bold letters:

> Where is the Mediterranean Sea on the world map?
>
> What conditions are found in the lands around it?
>
> What should we know about the land and people of Egypt?
>
> How did ancient people there contribute to our civilization?
>
> Write and send me questions you think we should answer about the Middle East.

Mrs. Snively then pinpointed the Middle East by identifying it as The Land of the Five Seas, The Bridge of Three Continents and The Crossroads of Three Continents. For each designation there was a cleanly drawn visual locating and naming the five seas, illustrating the bridging and intersecting of continents.

As the lesson continued she asked questions, pausing for the students to write answers to be checked later by the classroom teachers. As she outlined the areas to be covered during the following weeks of the Middle East unit, she illustrated life in the region with paintings of farming in ancient Egypt, Jesus' entry into Jerusalem and scenes from tales of the Arabian Nights. The television screen came alive with photographs of the Dead Sea Scrolls, pipelines carrying oil from the desert to the Mediterranean, Moslems at prayer, Arabs and Israelis at work, cars and sheep in the streets of modern Baghdad.

Having sketched a panorama of Middle Eastern life, Mrs. Snively urged students to learn the names and locations of its countries. As she mentioned Egypt and Syria, Turkey, Lebanon, Israel and the rest, the names appeared as if by magic on a blank map of the area. They had been placed on transparent overlays which were flipped into position at the precise moment by a TV crew member under instructions from the director in the control room.

After assigning her viewers pages from their textbook she asked them to include in their notes the answer to the question, "What is the Middle East?" Then she said, "Let's catch up on what's been happening recently in the Eastern Hemisphere so we can be well informed about these neighbors of ours."

With that cue, a newsreel film of recent developments in the Middle East was shown after which the TV lesson ended and the classroom teachers took over.

The classroom teachers, having watched the reactions of students to the telecast and noted the answers to questions, are able to gage the areas of difficulty and comprehension. In following up telecasts their ingenuity is given free rein. If class interest indicates the advisability of specializing in some phase of the topic there is adequate time and opportunity. Washington County's experience is that far from standardizing classroom procedures the telecasts stimulate greater adventures in learning. This is reflected by a marked increase in the use of school libraries and cultural resources throughout the community.

The television center has a videotape recorder. To overcome scheduling problems lessons can be taped while being shown to some groups and played back to later classes. This playback feature enables TV teachers to analyze their own performances and improve their presentations.

Television reaches more than 90 percent of Washington County students and stimulating guests who would not have time to visit 50 individual schools are quite willing to join studio teachers before the cameras. Scientists, artists, businessmen and statesmen have been brought into the county's classrooms, adding flavor and interest without increasing the budget.

Fourth grade social studies classes learning about wildlife of Washington County heard experts of Maryland's Inland Fish and Game Commission describe conservation practices and watched spellbound as they exhibited animals and birds brought to the studio. Apart from the factual knowledge they acquired, the youngsters gained insight into the humane treatment of animals. They were invited to visit fish hatcheries and game refuges and they learned about an interesting occupation.

Army officers flew to the studio by helicopter to assist in the teaching of mapreading, a DuPont chemist described the training needed for his field and a novelist discussed creative writing. Teenagers from 34 nations invited to the United States for a forum series, appeared before the Washington County cameras and provided more graphic evidence than textbooks of the need for world unity.

For all its wonder, television is used sparingly in Washington County. Only junior high school students receive as much as 80 minutes a day of TV programming. Elementary school students average 37 minutes, high schoolers 30 minutes a day.

Even this moderate use has resulted in a measurable improvement in education. While Washington County officials are unwilling to assess results until the completion of the five-year period in 1961, carefully conducted research studies offer convincing indication of television's rich potential.

Between September 1957 and May 1958, the achievement in mathematics of 5,645 pupils in grades 3 to 8 receiving instruction in television was compared to that of 3,740 students in non-TV classes. In the third grade forms A and B of the Science Research Associates Arithmetic Test were administered. Grades 4 through 8 received forms 1 and 2 of the arithmetic section of the Iowa Tests of Basic Skills. Form Z of the Cooperative Plane Geometry Test was also used.

The groups which received televised lessons outperformed the non-TV students at every grade level. The TV pupils in grades 3, 4, 5 and 6 exceeded the national norm in concepts. The sixth grade television group, 50 percent of whose members had received televised lessons in grade 5, surpassed the national norm to a greater extent than any other grade.

Some 1,465 sixth-graders were classified according to past achievements and IQ, and the achievement of those taking arithmetic by television was compared to that of the nontelevision group. During the 9-month period pupils with an average IQ of 99 who received televised instruction advanced 11 months in growth. The comparable non-TV group gained 5 months.

In a group of below-average students those receiving telecast lessons gained 11 months while the nontelevision pupils averaged a growth of 7 months.

Among the above-average pupils, the television group gained 10 months, the nontelevision students 9.

Among matched groups of students taking the Cooperative Plane Geometry Test, the television students ranked 22 percent higher on the national scale than the nontelevision pupils.

Gains in other subjects are equally impressive. On the Crary American History Test, a group of TV students in May 1958 scored 17 percent higher than a comparable group of non-TV students the previous year.

Washington County testing has established significant values in televised teaching to large classes. A television-taught class of 94 students in ninth grade science showed slightly greater growth in subject matter than a class of 53.

Three groups of American history students, one with 83 youngsters and two with 42 pupils each gained virtually the same ground academically. At a time of acute teacher shortage, the implications of successful teaching to over-size classes is obvious.

More detailed information on the testing program as well as other phases of closed-circuit TV is available from T. Wilson Cahall, television coordinator, Board of Education, Hagerstown, Md.

Less obvious but equally real advantages of television lie in the redeployment of teachers. Clear Spring High

School furnishes an example. Its television classes of 100 students in mathematics, science and core freed classroom teachers to organize a trigonometry class for 5 pupils and a journalism course for 14.

In Washington County, as in other sections of the United States, ancient stereotypes of uniform classroom size are beginning to break down.

In science, music, art, mathematics and foreign languages, where the scarcity of qualified teachers is most deeply felt, television has brought unique benefits to Washington County. In general science 1,900 seventh graders and 1,600 eighth graders receive televised lessons. These have revolutionized the countywide program, lifted the level of high school science and brought new adventure to the classroom.

Ralph Rohrbaugh, who teaches the course, has two assets lacked by all junior high teachers—time and equipment. In addition he has a scientific background and a love of subject matter shared by few teachers. Using a variety of electrical equipment, vacuum pumps, enlarged models, charts, films and ingenious personal demonstrations, he fascinates his youthful audience.

It takes Rohrbaugh an average of one hour to set up the apparatus for one TV class. To match two of his TV lessons, 20 equally qualified science teachers would each be required to teach five periods utilizing comparable equipment.

In music and art the advantages of televised teaching are even more apparent. The Washington County Board of Education has estimated that it would require 34 music and art teachers at a total annual salary of $171,000 to serve the elementary schools of the system. The teachers are not available. Instead two gifted music teachers and two artists provide televised lessons of exceptional quality. The artists are both professionals; one is director of Washington County's Museum of Fine Arts. As an indication of teaching effectiveness, more than 10,000 students viewed the school art exhibit at the museum which attracted a record number of entries from the television classes. Since televised art instruction was introduced the number of Washington County students who attend Saturday and Sunday art classes at the museum has reached a new high. The museum and the county library are linked within the television circuit.

As for mathematics, closed-circuit television has made school authorities realize the lengths to which youngsters can be challenged successfully. A voluntary TV class, Math for Mathematicians, attracts an average of 50 high school seniors at 8 o'clock each morning *before the start of regular classes*.

Taught by Jim Davis, whose scholarship to Case Institute of Technology last summer included training in electronic computers, Math for Mathematicians breaks high school barriers and introduces gifted students to analytics and calculus. The best qualified teacher for this course, Davis can reach every high school in the county only through the medium of television. He televises his lessons Monday, Wednesday and Friday and visits his students on Tuesday and Thursday. The 27 studio teachers visit classrooms as frequently as possible, bringing them into greater personal contact with students and teachers.

There are other points of contact, one of the most useful being the feedback card, sent by the classroom teacher to the studio teacher. The card has space for the teacher to comment on the clarity of picture and sound, the development of the lesson, the use of visuals, the speed of the lesson, vocabulary employed, class participation during and after the telecast. A blank side permits the classroom teacher to add other comments. Here are samples from actual feedback cards:

"The boys and girls of Fountaindale first grades would like you to know how very much they have enjoyed the enrichment programs this year. The teachers feel as though they have learned many things this year. Sincerely, First Grade Teachers."

"You captured their imagination with big new words (lever, inclined plane, ramp, pulley). For them it was very thought provoking. I have always felt science was my weakest point in teaching."

"I just wanted to tell you how pleased and grateful I feel that our pupils have the opportunity to be taught *Art* by an *Artist!*"

"I have never seen children so interested!"

At surprisingly rare intervals a feedback card like the following is sent to a TV teacher:

"Introduction: dull; vocabulary: too difficult; interest: average to low. The globe on the axis was rotated in the wrong direction. A graphic globe would have been better than a political one. Did you ask yourself: 'Just what do I want the first grade to learn from this lesson?'"

The feedback cards are virtually unanimous in agreeing that televised teaching has made possible the successful introduction of French in the fourth grade of Washington County schools. One week after school opened a visitor to a class in a rural school without its own French teacher was treated to a remarkable display of conversational fluency. Taught by the oral and aural method, without having read any French words in textbooks or on blackboards, the nine-year-olds worked easily with the TV teacher.

"Montrez-moi les yeux," said the pleasant young teacher on the television screen.

Each child pointed to his eyes.

"Qu'est-ce que c'est?" asked the teacher, holding up a ball.

"C'est une balle," replied the youngsters in unison.

"Qu'est-ce que c'est?" she asked, picking up a drawing of a little boy and pointing to his ears.

"Ce sont les oreilles," chirped the class.

Before the lesson the children had received a drawing of a clown's head with eyes, ears, nose and mouth omitted.

"Dessinez les yeux," said the teacher.

Small hands circled the eyes on the blank face.

"Dessinez le nez."

The clown's bulbous nose appeared.

"Dessinez la bouche."

The mouth spread from ear to ear in a grin.

One senses the growth of self-confidence and pride on the part of students during these brief TV segments which are limited to 10 minutes four times a week. Learning a foreign language in the same manner as they learned their own, the children mimic the teacher with expert facility.

In Washington County classroom and studio teachers are on an equal footing. Their pay is identical. Each regards the other as essential. Extensive surveys of classroom teachers whose anonymity assured frank answers, indicate the overwhelming support for the use of television.

Asked "Should part of the teaching of fifth grade social

studies be done by television," 94 percent of the teachers replied affirmatively.

Ninety-eight percent of the fourth grade social studies teachers replied "Yes" to the same question.

A survey of teacher opinion concerning televised arithmetic contained the following revealing responses:

Teachers who have previously taught arithmetic without television now prefer to teach it	GRADES				
	1-2	3	4	5	6
With help of a studio teacher	77%	75%	86%	89%	79%
Without help of a studio teacher	23%	25%	14%	11%	21%

Other surveys have confirmed classroom teacher acceptance of televised reading programs.

Ninety percent of all teachers in television schools replied anonymously to a questionnaire on their attitudes toward televised teaching. Here are the percentages answering three key questions:

1. Do you regard teaching with the aid of television as:

83% a stimulating adventure in education

9% no different than before

5% an unpleasant experience

3% other comments

2. Would you prefer to teach the class you are now teaching without the aid of televised instruction, or would you prefer the aid of television?

83% with the aid of television

17% without the aid of television

3. Do you believe that television can improve the quality of instruction in our schools?

89% yes

10% no

1% other comments

Five hundred twenty families living in the area covered by the closed-circuit TV system were interviewed by phone or in person to determine community attitudes about the experiment. Seventy-eight percent responded favorably. In a subsequent question, however, 30 percent stated that if given a choice they would prefer their children to take lessons *without* television. Industrial and business leaders who personally saw TV teaching in action responded to the same questions with greater enthusiasm. Ninety-six percent responded favorably, 89 percent felt that the use of television would help to improve education and 75 percent stated that if given a choice they would prefer their children to take lessons with television.

One reason for the strong acceptance of television in Washington County may lie in the experiment's use of local talent only. All studio teachers spring from the school system. The camera crews consist of students at Hagerstown Junior College who are paid $1 an hour except while earning credit in television courses.

With but two exceptions the studio directors are also Junior College students. The exceptions are a local radio announcer who works part-time at the television center and the production supervisor, who has both commercial and educational television experience. The only other outsiders in the project are the chief engineer and his assistant. There is no "show business" aura to the programming or the atmosphere. The studio teacher determines the manner in which the lesson is to be taught and the director and crews handle the technical details. The studio teachers become familiarized with procedures and equipment in a summer training program during which they are paid their regular salaries.

The visual aids which contribute so much to the televised lessons are prepared by three 19-year-olds who are paid $1.40 an hour for their services. Former art students in Washington County high schools, they exemplify the homegrown talent that exists in every community. Working closely with studio teachers they have developed techniques of illustration, lettering and model-building which will be invaluable to school systems launching similar programs.

Washington County's closed-circuit system is a pioneer technically as well as educationally. A cable, slightly larger than a pen and "filled with intelligence," carries six sound and six picture signals 80 miles from the six studios of the television center in Hagerstown to the 37 schools within the circuit. The strength of the signal is boosted by amplifiers within the line so picture and sound are uniformly clear throughout the county. Lessons and films are transmitted over six channels to some 600 standard television receivers in the classrooms. Unlike open-circuit television home TV sets cannot tune to these channels.

Washington County was selected as the site of the most elaborate experiment of its kind because of a happy coincidence. In assessing the best possible educational program for the future, its school officials were investigating possible uses of television at the same time that the Fund for the Advancement of Education and the Radio-Electronics-

Television Manufacturers Association (RETMA) sought an appropriate school system for a pilot TV project. They invited the Washington County school system to present a proposal for such a program. Submitted in May 1956, it suggested a five-year project beginning in September 1956. The proposal was accepted.

Now an intensive, countywide effort began. About 100 teachers, principals, PTA leaders, supervisors and consultants held a six-week workshop beginning July 9 to complete plans for the project. They agreed that with television you probably:

COULD	COULD NOT
Motivate and stimulate	Handle classroom discussion
Inform	
Demonstrate	Clear up misunderstanding
Develop ideas	Provide for followup of lesson
Show application	
Enrich backgrounds	Direct and supervise the activities growing out of the lesson
Provide common experiences	
Suggest activities	Help pupils apply what has been learned
Challenge pupils to assume more responsibility for their own study	

This analysis resulted in a team approach with the studio teacher scheduled to handle instruction best suited to television and the classroom teacher responsible for the areas best suited to personal contact. Classroom and studio teachers worked together to prepare the guide material which was a natural outgrowth of the curriculum studies which had been under way since 1948. In preparing for

96

the common experience of television, teachers unified the curriculum for the entire county, an accomplishment which has resulted in unending bonuses. The joint effort of teachers, parents and administrators which preceded the introduction of television revitalized education in Washington County, toughened the program and led to the general realization that pupils could be challenged by more wideranging and demanding courses of instruction.

As the workshop tackled the substance of education, a "crash" program to obtain and install equipment was launched by a committee representing RETMA, the Chesapeake and Potomac Telephone Co. and individual electronic firms. On July 15 there was no equipment. Fifty-eight days later, on September 11, a televised lesson in senior English inaugurated transmission over the circuit.

The Fund for the Advancement of Education had made initial grants of $108,000 to plan the experiment, train personnel to administer and supervise the program and carry out its evaluation. Seventy firms affiliated with RETMA (which is now called the Electronic Industries Association) provided about $300,000 worth of cameras, lights, studio equipment and television receivers. The telephone company, with the assistance of Bell Laboratories, developed the closed-circuit system, installed the cable, transmission and distribution facilities. It provided these services without charge for the first two years utilizing the experience to determine the rates for future closed-circuit rentals.

Collectively the contributions to Washington County are estimated to total approximately one million dollars. This is a huge sum but only one-third the cost of one new Hagerstown high school.

Superintendent Brish expects Washington County to continue its TV program when the Ford grants (which have totaled over $700,000) expire in 1961. On the basis of three years' experience he has developed figures to justify the economy of closed-circuit TV.

Washington County schools will require 32 fewer teachers because of large-class viewing. The saving of $180,000 a year in teacher salaries covers the entire annual cost of television including the telephone company's cable charges.

This saving in salaries is *not* at the expense of qualified teachers. It means simply that Washington County will not be forced, as in the past, to hire unqualified, new teachers to fill the gap caused by retirement, marriage or resignation. There will still be a need for competent new teachers.

Closed-circuit television has brought other economic advantages. Superintendent Brish estimates that it would cost $245,000 to duplicate the French, reading skills, special education and advanced mathematics, now taught by television. This is apart from the $171,000 saved by the televised teaching of music and art.

Much of the credit for the success of the Hagerstown experiment should go to the quiet, relaxed man who harnessed teachers, students and parents for this effort. Superintendent Brish has gained their confidence because he regards television as only one tool—highly useful, enormously potential—but only one tool in the educational process.

"First decide what sort of education you want for your youngsters," he says, "then find out how television can *help* you to reach that goal."

For further information about the Washington County project contact:

> T. Wilson Cahall
> Television Coordinator
> Board of Education
> Hagerstown, Md.

For another approach to educational television see chapter 8—The Electronic Link: Television in Southwestern Indiana, p. 143, and for related experimental programs see Appendix, pp. 179–80.

6. *Experiments in Excellence:*

EVANSTON (ILL.) TOWNSHIP HIGH SCHOOL
GOLDEN (COLO.) HIGH SCHOOL

There are 8,100,000 high school students in the United States. It is estimated that in 10 years this number will rise to 11,664,000. How do the high schools propose to meet the challenge of quality and quantity?

Our secondary schools have not been adventurous. They have often failed to exploit the potential of their students. The era of outer space has caused a great threshing-about in science but few high schools have examined their total programs critically.

Evanston (Ill.) Township High School and Golden (Colo.) High School represent a growing number of secondary schools which are experimenting in their organization and curriculum to meet the challenges of a new decade.

ON THE SURFACE THERE IS LITTLE
similarity between Evanston (Ill.) Township High School
and Golden (Colo.) High School. Evanston, population
75,000, is a wealthy suburb of Chicago. Its high school has
a 75-year tradition of excellence and the $750 annual cost-
per-pupil of its 3,600 students is among the Nation's
highest.

Golden, population 6,000, is in the foothills of the Rocky
Mountains. It is best known as the burial place of Buffalo
Bill. Its high school was built in 1957 and the $367 cost-
per-pupil of its 550 students is modest.

For all these differences, Evanston and Golden have
many things in common. They share a restlessness to experiment with the new and hopeful. They distrust self-
satisfaction and smugness. They look upon education as
an adventure, capable of unearthing hidden treasures in
people as well as ideas. They fear that the rigidity of high
school schedules, unimaginative courses and standard class
size will lead to hardening of the educational arteries.

Dr. James B. Conant has pointed out the difficulties
of providing a complete secondary education in a small

school. At the opposite extreme, bigness has its problems too.

Evanston's student body mushroomed from 2,100 in 1949 to its present enrollment of 3,600. Superintendent-Principal Dr. Lloyd S. Michael and his faculty feared that this expansion would make impossible a continuance of the individual attention that had characterized their school. Their answer: "schools within a school."

Evanston Township High School now consists of four separate divisions, each virtually a school in itself. Each division of approximately 900 students contains one-fourth of the 9th, 10th, 11th and 12th graders. They are selected at random and are of varied ability.

Each "school within the school" is headed by a division principal with four assistants, one each for freshmen, sophomores, juniors and seniors. Each grade level within the division contains from 225 to 250 students and has its own qualified guidance counselor. One school social worker is assigned to each division to handle cases referred by the counselors. Intramural and club activities are carried on within the division framework. It is thus similar to the college "house plan."

Parent meetings are also centered in the division providing a more closely knit union of parents, teachers, students and administrators than would exist in a school of 3,600.

"The school within a school" organization has enabled Evanston to fuse the advantages of a small student body with the superior educational values of a large plant with its well-developed laboratories and cultural assets. The academic faculty is not divided between divisions but serves everyone.

This reorganization has opened new career lines for the

division principals, enabling them to earn higher salaries as administrators without losing touch with students. School purchasing and details of physical plant are handled centrally at Evanston permitting the division principal to concentrate on education.

"My basic interest is these youngsters," says Walter Rasmussen, one of the division principals. "I'm not interested in building maintenance, the costs of running the cafeteria and such matters and under this system I'm spared those details."

Each week Rasmussen and the other division principals meet with Dr. Michael, their superintendent-principal. This organization lightens Dr. Michael's burdens, speeds communication within the school and enables individual teachers to make creative contributions which would otherwise be stalled by bureaucracy.

One thousand miles westward Golden High School has devised other techniques to lift the dead hand of bureaucracy.

It is participating in the experimental programs of the National Association of Secondary-School Principals, a department of the National Education Association. The principals have established a Commission on the Experimental Study of the Utilization of the Staff in the Secondary School (there have been no experiments in short titles). This commission has launched a concerted campaign against standpattism. Its director is J. Lloyd Trump, formerly professor of education at the University of Illinois, and its chairman is Evanston's Dr. Lloyd S. Michael!

The commission has an eager participant in Golden. The Colorado community is in Jefferson County's School District R-1, one of the Nation's most advanced systems. Under the inexhaustible leadership of its superintendent, Dr. Robert H. Johnson, Jefferson County has introduced pace-setting foreign language and science programs ranging from kindergarten through high school. Each of the eight high schools in the District is experimenting in different aspects of team teaching. Golden has concentrated on flexible class size and flexible scheduling as its share of the countywide ferment.

Classes of unconventional size have been accepted casually at Golden since Jefferson County conducted its extensive "Class-Size Study" in 1957–58. This carefully controlled experiment attempted to determine the effects of the number of students in a classroom on achievement, attitude and behavior of the learners. It involved 1,075 10th and 11th grade students in English, plane geometry, biology and American history. The experimental classes contained 10, 20, 35, 60, 70 and 70-plus students. Iowa Tests of Educational Development established that all classes were academically similar except for groups of superior students who comprised separate classes of different sizes.

One teacher was assigned to the classes with 35 or fewer students. Two teachers met the larger groups except in two cases where a clerk-assistant and an uncertificated teacher joined a fully qualified teacher.

During the 33d and 34th weeks of the term all participating students were tested. The results revealed that "other factors being equivalent, the number of learners in a teaching-learning situation is insignificant." There was no significant difference of achievement between academically similar classes of different size. The achievement of the large groups led to the conclusion that team teaching can help to solve the problems caused by increased enrollment, a shortage of qualified teachers and the physical limitation of conventional classrooms.

The fact that small groups of superior students did not outperform large groups of the gifted resulted in the conclusion that "small grouping of identified high capacity learners is not academically nor economically feasible."

Having hurdled the barriers of rigid class size, Golden and Jefferson County turned their attention to rigid scheduling.

All over America high schools schedule students to take the same subject for the same duration of time at the same period five times a week. Variations based on differences of subject matter are virtually nonexistent.

In spite of this tradition, there is no evidence to prove that teaching French I to 32 pupils Monday to Friday in room 16 is necessarily the most effective method. It does, however, simplify the life of the man responsible for organizing the schedule. Assuming that the purposes of education may be more profound, Golden and other high schools are examining alternatives to this uniformity.

Most high school teachers handle five classes a day with one free period. Art Papenfus, Golden's biology teacher, is free during the first, second, third, fourth and sixth periods on Monday. During the fifth period he lectures to all 180 biology students in the auditorium. He uses the overhead projector to outline his talk and he utilizes films, slides and filmstrips. A dynamic lecturer, he holds his audience's interest with apparent ease.

At the large-group sessions Papenfus introduces new topics, presents overviews and conducts reviews. There are two each week. During the remaining biology periods, the students are divided into six smaller groups. Here the premium is on give-and-take as teacher and pupils break down the material covered in the large-class lecture.

One of the biology students analyzed the success of large-group lectures in these words:

"Imagine a guy repeating the same lecture six times to six different classes. It would be different each time and by the time he got to the end of the day the last class would suffer because of his exhaustion. This way he has time to do a terrific job of preparation and he can give it everything he has. If he knocks himself out he's got a free period later to recover."

Mr. Papenfus has a total of *nine* free periods during the week. He takes advantage of this freedom in a manner which benefits all his students. As the winner of two National Science Foundation Fellowships and an Esso Foundation Award, he has taken advanced courses at Denver University, Colorado State University and the University of Colorado. During free periods he often visits these science departments to keep abreast of new developments.

Recently he obtained reproductions of superbly executed ancient anatomical drawings from the University of Colorado. Transparencies were then prepared for viewing on the overhead projector and students saw their subject in a new dimension. In the usual teaching schedule Papenfus would have little or no time for personal research.

Golden's biology students study in large and small groups. They meet four times a week instead of daily, and classes take place at different times. A typical student has large classes the fifth period Monday and Friday, a small class the fourth period Tuesday, and laboratory the third and fourth periods on Thursday.

Golden has experimented successfully with team teaching in English. Four teachers handled 180 sophomores, rotating large-class lectures to take advantage of teaching strengths. Mrs. Epis concentrated on art and its influence, Mr. Elliott on literature, Miss Schmidtberger on speech, dramatics and poetry, and Mr. Coon on other lands and other customs. Their paperwork was handled by an instruction assistant who was paid the same wage as clerical employees.

All this is highly unconventional but it is not Golden's only escape from orthodoxy. Another form of heresy is the double period which Golden has experimented with in English, social studies, mathematics, foreign languages, business education, music, art and homemaking.

Among Golden's physics, chemistry and biology teachers there is agreement that two successive periods of laboratory work are more than twice as effective as single periods.

"Students are not as rushed during the double period," says chemistry teacher Christensen. "The waste motion in setting up apparatus and cleaning up is minimized by the extended period. I have much more opportunity to give them individual attention and there are fewer incomplete experiments."

The double period also makes more feasible science field trips and visits to industrial plants.

Golden's chemistry teacher reports that the combination of the double lab and the use of semimicrochemistry have revolutionized class performance. In this system each student has a complete kit of chemicals and experiments are scaled down to utilize small quantities. Endless trooping to the storeroom and consequent waste of time have ended.

Only about 10 percent of U.S. high schools have adopted this technique.

Golden is helping to solve other problems. The U.S. Office of Education reports that only one in seven high school students studies a modern foreign language. Golden offers four years of Spanish, French, Latin and Russian. Jefferson County's three Russian teachers circuit ride its eight high schools. They are symptomatic of the enthusiasm for foreign languages generated by Superintendent Johnson.

Jefferson County high school enrollment in languages has risen 34 percent during the past year. This was stimulated by the introduction of Spanish as a required course from kindergarten through the sixth grade. Intensive in-service courses trained over 500 Jefferson County teachers in the aural-oral method of teaching Spanish. From kindergarten through the second grade only the hearing and speaking skills are practiced. "Thereafter," says Paul McRill, who directs the program, "at all levels, in a new unit of work the student first hears the new language patterns, then learns to read what he has learned to say and lastly learns to write what he has learned to read."

Jefferson County mirrors the experience of many communities which have introduced foreign languages at the elementary school level. It is hard to find an example of failure and children of all ability levels respond with enthusiasm.

Youngsters from the elementary schools of towns like Golden are revitalizing foreign languages in the high schools.

Language laboratories have been ordered for all the high schools of Jefferson County and the students of Golden are looking forward to their installation. If the experience of the language students of Evanston Township High School is any criterion, Golden boys and girls are in for a treat.

The more than 80 percent of Evanston Township High School students who study French, German, Latin, Spanish or Russian utilize one of the finest language laboratories in the United States. Built at a cost of $15,000, it consists of 36 soundproofed booths. Here students wear headphones in which they can hear either the teacher or recordings from a master console. Each booth has a microphone and button controls which enable the pupil to record, play back and erase his voice.

Here he can listen to tapes which have been made in conjunction with language textbooks. These have master portions spoken by native linguists which cannot be erased and blank portions for student fill-in. Playback permits him to compare his pronunciation with that of the native. The student fill-in can then be erased.

At the console the teacher can listen to, interrupt and converse with any pupil.

In foreign languages, as in other subjects, Evanston has an extensive honors program. Before Sputnik, before the publication of the Conant Report, the Killian Report and the Rockefeller Brothers study, *The Pursuit of Excellence,* Evanston Township High School had placed its highest premium on intellectual achievement. In Evanston excellence has not merely been pursued—it has been captured.

The Killian Report, *Education for the Age of Science,* states, "Talented students should be recognized at an early age and given guidance and counsel in planning their educational programs and in preparing for and choosing college and university work."

In Evanston gifted pupils like Peter de Lissavoy are

spotted early and given rich opportunities to make the most of their talents. He is now a high school senior but in the second grade of elementary school Peter's teacher had noted on his report card, "His keen interest in all subjects has been a pleasure to the room. I know that he will continue to show the same superior work and attitude in the third grade."

By the sixth grade Peter had scored among the top 4 percent of students nationally in the Stanford Achievement Test. In his final year of junior high school he improved on this score in a battery of achievement tests. The testing program has been worked out cooperatively by the junior and senior high school counselors. This coordination enables the latter to prepare the schedules of incoming students. In the transition from junior to senior high school, students who have shown academic promise are recognized immediately. They are ticketed as early as possible for honors courses and regarded as potential candidates for college level subjects.

In the case of Peter de Lissavoy this meant a ninth grade program of challenging quality. As a freshman he joined the 25 percent of Evanston students enrolled in the mathematics honors program. This has existed for more than 20 years. Pete's ninth grade honors course included advanced algebra not usually given until the third year.

In addition to honors mathematics Peter's freshman program consisted of sophomore biology, an honors course combining civics and world history instead of ordinary civics, English and technical arts.

The moment Pete de Lissavoy entered Evanston Township High School he became conscious of its focus on intellect. Years ago, when Evanston was a tightly knit, upper income community, its high school had established rigorous standards of scholarship and conduct. It had the atmosphere of a great private school. Today Evanston's diverse student body represents a cross section of economic, racial and religious backgrounds.

If anything Evanston is better than ever. Its students continue to win more than their share of National Merit Scholarships, creative writing prizes and Westinghouse Science Talent Awards.

One hundred seniors turned out on a Sunday afternoon for a poetry recital by E. E. Cummings, there are new exhibits of fine arts in the corridors every two weeks and the high school is one of a handful in the U.S. with a composer-in-residence.

Pete de Lissavoy has flourished in this atmosphere. The clean-cut 16-year-old son of a typographical designer, has made a distinguished record in the humanities as well as the sciences.

Malcolm Mosing, who taught one of his three honors English classes says, "Pete's essay, 'Why I Want To Be a Mathematician,' described the beauty of mathematics as an art and I regard it as a classic of its type. But Pete's term paper on 'Modern Tragedy' was equally impressive.

"This school," continues Mosing, "has never downgraded its humanities and there is no conflict between science and English. Our science teachers show their interest in literature, drama and music and I think our students try to emulate the well-rounded adult. Boys like Pete excel in a variety of disciplines."

After completing honors courses in English, physical science, world history and German, and college level work in algebra and trigonometry, Pete de Lissavoy was chosen for a rare honor.

The Pomfret School of Pomfret, Conn., selected seven students from leading school systems to join three of its African Studies pupils on a trip to Kenya, Central Africa, The Union of South Africa and Ghana. The Evanston faculty chose de Lissavoy and in the summer of 1959 he set out on his greatest adventure.

The journey had a profound effect upon Pete. It added fuel to a fire which had started burning with his honors courses in 10th and 11th grade English and in an honors program in world history. Suddenly science seemed less important. The literary gifts he had displayed in his essay on the beauty of mathematics flowered in his descriptions of the newly emerging nations of Africa.

In this, his senior year at Evanston, Pete de Lissavoy has altered his plans to become a pure mathematician. He hopes to go on to Harvard, major in political science and minor in journalism. At a time when science has become the be-all and end-all of so many high school programs for the gifted, Evanston's inspired teaching and rich curriculum are encouraging his new ambition.

At this critical moment of intellectual growth Peter has been given an opportunity which few high schools can offer. Along with the upper third of his senior class he is enrolled in humanities 4. This program is a breakaway from the compartmentalized study of English. In the words of Evanston's Annual Report it treats "in all possible depth those epochs of Western man from which have come our patterns of living in the 20th century. The term 'humanities' implies, of course, not just a consideration of literature but also an investigation of scientific, artistic and philosophic concepts and ideas, all of which are inextricably bound together to form our heritage of life patterns."

The reading ranges from *Prometheus Bound* and *Agamemnon* of ancient Greece through the great works of the Middle Ages; Petrarch, Shakespeare and the humanism of the Renaissance; the poets and essayists of the Age of Reason, and the novels, short stories, poetry and plays of the 20th century. The artistic development of Michelangelo, Bach and Beethoven and the concepts of Newton, Darwin and Einstein are also sketched.

Three hundred twenty seniors taking humanities 4 are instructed by a team of five teachers. Three of them prepare large-group lectures for two classes of 160 pupils each. The lecturers divide the subject matter in accordance with their own talents. They present this material to the large groups twice only. Relieved of repeating the talks frequently to smaller classes they gain the free time required for adequate preparation of future lectures.

All 5 teachers handle smaller groups ranging from 16 students for discussion, to 32 for supervised writing. An assistant handles clerical duties for the project and supervises study and research groups of 80.

It is not merely students of the caliber of Pete de Lissavoy who benefit from enlightenment at Evanston. Four teachers and 360 below-average, average and above-average students comprise the junior English team-teaching program. The size of the group varies with the lesson. About every 10 days, each of 3 groups of 120 hears a lecture which may be enhanced by the use of closed-circuit television, films or the Vu-graph transparency projector. Whatever the visual aids the sessions derive their excitement primarily from the skill of Evanston's English teachers. They are eloquent and unabashedly emotional in their presentations.

"When the bomb was dropped on Hiroshima," said Ned Hoopes in a hushed voice pointing to a huge blowup of an atomic explosion, "our relationship to man changed."

The 120-man class sat in rigid concentration as Mr. Hoopes, his voice charged with tension, analyzed the decision to drop the bomb and related it to John Hersey's *Hiroshima*.

His talk, punctuated by frequent literary, poetic and historic references reflected wide research among a variety of sources. The lecture was compelling because of the teacher's conviction and skill of delivery, characteristics too infrequently found in high school English classes.

"We hope," says English Chairman Clarence W. Hach, "that students will catch some of this fire."

They do, the slower students as well as the gifted. "It's fashionable here to study," said one youngster with a slight smile as if he himself could not believe what he was saying.

The selection of a student for honors or advanced placement at Evanston is equivalent to nomination for all-State halfback at most schools. There are honors classes in all departments of the high school. Selection is based on many factors. Test scores are not regarded as sacrosanct and every honors section has students who have revealed abilities to teachers which have escaped the surveillance of testing.

Evanston was one of the pilot schools in the College Entrance Examination Board's Advanced Placement Program. This permits gifted high school students to take college level courses in 11 subjects. The program culminates in rigorous examinations prepared by the College Board.

Colleges then consider the records of successful students for credit and advanced placement.

When the program began in 1953–54, 18 high schools, 532 students and 94 colleges participated. In 1958–59, 3,715 students at 355 high schools took examinations for 279 colleges. Among these were 57 Evanston students who took 115 examinations. Of these, 38 earned advanced placement in at least one subject and both advanced placement and college credit were granted in 22 cases.

Pete de Lissavoy has studied three college level courses, two in mathematics and one in United States history.

"The teachers I've had and the courses I've taken at Evanston," he says, "have gotten *everything* out of me."

Though Pete has shifted his emphasis from science to the humanities, his school offers the budding scientist matchless opportunities.

"Science at Evanston Township High School is for everyone," states the science department's bulletin, "the most strongly academic student, the average and even the pupil of low ability."

For the latter and those who are not bound for college there are several courses which "aim to introduce pupils to concepts of 'scientific method,' give useful and practical knowledge, and provide for general cultural values."

For the talented there are such innovations as the mathematics-science seminar.

In 1959 there were 3 seminar sections with a total of 44 students meeting every other day. For the first four to six weeks of the program a teacher-sponsor presents advanced aspects of mathematics and science. Students then select individual projects and choose areas in which *they* will teach their classmates. The teacher-sponsor becomes equivalent to a director of research. The seminar elects a student chairman and a librarian to circulate a wide range of published materials.

All topics considered are outside the range of established courses. Students have access to university libraries in the area and to professional specialists in their field of interest.

At the students' disposal is a new research laboratory which may be unmatched among the Nation's high schools and a library of 28,000 volumes.

The material quality of its plant has not induced smugness in Evanston. The high school has participated actively in the experiments of the Commission on the Experimental Study of the Utilization of the Staff in the Secondary School. In 1956–57 these experiments included the teaching of beginning typing and English-speech by closed-circuit television.

The typing teacher, two television cameras manned by trained volunteers and half the 70-student class were in the originating room. The rest of the class was in another room one floor away supervised by a clerical aide skilled in typing. A monitoring camera in the second room enabled the television teacher to see the activity in this class as well as in the originating room. A third volunteer acted as "director" from a nearby booth. Here he could control the switching from camera to camera for the most effective picture.

Television proved effective in focusing student attention on typing techniques.

A talk-back system in both rooms enabled students to ask and the teacher to answer questions at any time. The clerical assistant aided students in her room and handled the class paperwork.

118

Careful evaluation of student records indicated that the television classes "attained skill in typing comparable to that of students taught in nontelevision courses." In every area of evaluation the televised teaching was judged as effective as conventional instruction though only one qualified teacher was required for 70 students.

In the second television experiment three sections of English-speech, a sophomore elective, were taught in three adjoining rooms by one television teacher assisted by two cadet teachers from Northwestern University. The groups rotated so that they were in the originating room with the teacher every third day. Again a talk-back system permitted questions and answers to be heard in all rooms at any time. Students telecast scenes from plays, conducted interviews related to the course material, participated in panel discussions and watched films of the Elizabethan theater on their TV receivers.

An intensive effort to evaluate the program by outside consultants as well as Evanston personnel indicated satisfactory achievement by students. Their final marks were comparable to those obtained by students in the nontelevised class of the previous year. Television students made at least as high marks on the schoolwide spring examination in written composition as had their nontelevision predecessors. Although there were also some limitations in the television teaching, the staff concluded that "with the help of television and cadet teachers, the English-speech teacher was able to instruct three groups of students in one period without lowering the school's expected standards of high levels of achievement and fruitful learning conditions."

Evanston has utilized television in other ways. Large

groups of biology students have seen dissections magnified for clear viewing by a TV camera located directly above the experiment. Instructions in the use of the library were telecast simultaneously to all freshman English students instead of repetitive talks by the librarian.

All Evanston homerooms are equipped with television receivers and the closed-circuit is used as a public address system. Student council election campaigns, musical programs and skits have been transmitted to all students at one time.

Future television projects involve enrichment classes in art, homemaking, English, social studies, mathematics and science.

The closed-circuit television experiments are the only Evanston programs aided financially by the Commission on the Experimental Study of the Utilization of the Staff in the Secondary School.

The grants made by the commission to Golden High School were for research and evaluation. The experiments themselves added no cost to the school system.

In its modest grants to schools like Evanston and Golden the commission has made deep inroads on national apathy. J. Lloyd Trump, the commission's director, has written two pamphlets, *New Horizons for Secondary School Teachers* and *Images of the Future,* which state the case for change with clarity and force. The latter booklet is available free of charge from the commission's offices at 200 Gregory Hall, Urbana, Ill.

The Fund for the Advancement of Education and the Ford Foundation have supported the commission's work with grants in excess of $1,000,000 but the program is administered entirely by the National Association of

Secondary-School Principals, whose Bulletins of January 1958, 1959 and 1960 contain detailed descriptions of many of the experimental projects.

In *New Horizons for Secondary School Teachers*, Dr. Trump writes, "The shortage of teachers will become worse rather than better in the years ahead. The alternatives are clear. School systems that cling to traditional ways of doing things will face the necessity of hiring progressively poorer teachers. Those that exercise imagination and ingenuity may cause the quality of education to rise with enrollments."

Evanston and Golden educators are exercising that imagination and ingenuity. How many other high school administrators are willing to take a fresh look at their problems?

For further information about the Commission on the Experimental Study of the Utilization of the Staff in the Secondary School contact:

> J. Lloyd Trump
> National Association of
>   Secondary-School Principals
> 1201 16th St., NW
> Washington 6, D.C.

For further information about Golden High School and Jefferson County schools contact:

> Dr. Robert H. Johnson, Superintendent
> Jefferson County School District R-1
> 1580 Yarrow St.
> Lakewood, Colo.

For further information about Evanston Township High School contact:

> Dr. Lloyd S. Michael
> Superintendent-Principal
> Evanston Township High School
> Evanston, Ill.

For related experimental programs see Appendix, pp. 180–87.

7. *Breaking the Rural Barrier:*

THE CATSKILL PROJECT

Should a youngster be penalized because he is born in a rural instead of an urban area? Obviously he should not. But rural schools face difficult problems.

It is difficult to attract good teachers to sparsely settled areas. It is difficult to equip a small school to do the same job as a large school. It is difficult to provide the same challenge to small numbers of talented pupils.

The first and foremost solution is the consolidation of school districts. The merging of these small units leads to larger, better-equipped schools, more capable of attracting competent teachers. In 1948 there were about 102,000 U.S. school districts. Today the number has dropped to about 45,000. During the past 10 years the number of districts in New York State has been reduced from 3,400 to about 1,300.

Unfortunately there are limits to consolidation. Several experimental programs are tackling the problem of rural schools which for geographic and other reasons have not consolidated. In New York State, the Catskill Area Project in Small School Design has made promising headway.

EVERY SATURDAY MORNING AT 6:30 the alarm clock awakens a 17-year-old high school senior named Evelyn Fairbairn. Then she is driven over 50 miles of mountain road from her father's dairy farm near Margaretville, N.Y., to the State University College of Education at Oneonta.

"It's the most exciting day of my week," she says. Evelyn is 1 of 90 "able and ambitious" students from 27 Catskill Mountain schools participating in a program to lift the level of rural education. Known as the Catskill Area Project in Small School Design, its results will have important implications for the 17,000 of 21,000 U.S. high schools which Dr. James B. Conant considers too small to be effective.

Last year Evelyn Fairbairn participated in the weekly mathematics seminar at Oneonta under the direction of James Burling, an assistant professor at the college.

"She was interested in everything under the sun," he recalls. "Among other things we touched upon Boolean algebra, in which one deals with collections of abstract things instead of numbers. We talked about set theory, which usually is reserved for graduate students, introduced calculus and had some fun with number theory. Like the other high school youngsters at the seminar, Evelyn was head and shoulders above most of my college students as a mathematician."

Evelyn is president of the student association of Margaretville Central School, sings in the school chorus and received the highest State musical rating as a flutist. There are only 145 students in her high school and the average graduating class numbers 25, 75 below the Conant minimum.

Seminars for "the able and ambitious" reflect only one phase of the Catskill Project, which is designed to improve the quality of rural education for slow and average as well as superior students.

A vital force in the origination of the project is Dr. Frank W. Cyr, a Nebraskan who is professor of education at Teachers College, Columbia University. He is a dedicated believer in the unique qualities of the rural school. At Margaretville Central School he expounded his philosophy.

"We've got to have some small communities and small organizations in this country. We need the strength that comes from diversity. All of us favor school consolidation when it is practicable but there are climatic and geographical problems that often prevent it. We can't just abolish 17,000 small high schools. I'm not opposed to bigness—I just want to make smallness more productive. Look out there! Can you imagine a healthier setting for a school?"

Through the window Mount Pakatakan loomed 3,000 feet above the school, its forested slopes bright in the sunlight.

"This is the challenge," Cyr continued. "Can we give the 145 youngsters in Margaretville the same variety of subjects as the kids get in New York City? If we can, we've got something."

Supported by grants from the Fund for the Advancement of Education, 27 schools in a tricounty dairy farming area are attempting to meet the challenge. Cyr is executive secretary of the project, but the plan is homegrown, and applicable to any rural region.

The small high school suffers from too few students, too few teachers. Many courses are denied youngsters because classes would be too small to justify the hiring of a teacher —if a qualified teacher were available. To overcome these obstacles the Catskill Project has experimented with multiple class teaching, supervised correspondence courses, electronic and human aides, the sharing of specialist teachers and flexible scheduling.

Tom Matalavage is a Margaretville mathematics teacher with a typical rural dilemma—how to teach two classes at the same time. Seventeen freshmen enrolled for elementary algebra and five requested general mathematics in his one free period. Instead of eliminating one course he teaches both in the same classroom simultaneously.

This is possible because Tom prepared learner's guides for each group, enabling the students to work independently. In the introduction he wrote:

> "With this guide and your textbook you have the tools needed for the successful completion of the course. Your teacher will provide you with the opportunity to learn and with whatever guidance you might need. If you have questions about directions, new words, or solutions of problems ask your teacher about them or you might find the

> assistance you need from some member of your class."

The two groups work separately, each following its own guide. The guides spell out the objectives of the courses and specify the use of textbooks and other materials.

As his students work, Matalavage circulates and is available for assistance. When it becomes necessary for him to present new material he finds that he can talk to the 17 without disturbing the 5 and vice versa. He cites unexpected bonuses in the assumption of new responsibilities by his students.

"This is learning by discovery," says Matalavage enthusiastically, "and it seems to work. Apart from the fact that they seem to be learning mathematics I don't think you can measure their personal growth—in self-discipline and the ability to work together."

From a practical standpoint Tom has more time to devote to the slower learners in the class.

"Frankly," he says, "I was extremely doubtful about teaching more than one class when this project started. Now I'm convinced that I can teach *three* classes simultaneously—elementary and intermediate algebra and general mathematics."

Laverne Thomas of Franklin Central School has added another dimension to the teaching of multiple classes. In addition to preparing learner's guides he has tape recorded his lectures and instructions. He has taught intermediate algebra, trigonometry and advanced mathematics simultaneously and the record of his students on the New York State Regents examinations bears out his confidence in the technique.

Thomas works at the chalkboard with one group while the two other classes in the room receive their lectures and instructions from the tape recorder.

"Tape is an extension of the teacher," he says, "and the guides unify the courses by referring students to the textbook or to the tape recording for explanation and commentary. Meanwhile I'm available for consultation by anyone having difficulty."

Multiple classes have worked successfully in business courses. In one room seniors in vocational business carry out an assignment by taking dictation from a transcriber, typing, cutting stencils and doing business arithmetic. Meanwhile, in another part of the same room, their teacher is instructing ninth graders in typing.

English and social studies, art and foreign languages also have been taught in multiple classes.

Margaret Law, a language teacher of Franklin Central School, is a notable pioneer in this technique. In one room she teaches Latin to one group while advanced French students sit before a tape recorder listening to the conversation of natives. In another corner the lone girl who chose German studies a correspondence course complete with tapes. Miss Law finds time to check on her progress too.

The use of supervised correspondence courses is an integral part of the Catskill Project. Launched by the Chautauqua Institute in the 1890's, study by correspondence has become a significant educational tool.

One university's correspondence program enrolls almost 10,000 students in the United States and 75 countries. Some correspondence programs are supplemented by magnetic tapes, phonograph records and personal communications between instructor and student.

Schools of Tomorrow—Today!

Universities and private correspondence schools offer more than 400 courses on the high school level. Seventy-five percent of the students who begin the courses complete them. Schools in the Catskill Project report that talented students, seeking to enlarge their horizons beyond the school curriculum, are most likely to request study by correspondence.

One Margaretville High School senior had exhausted all the mathematics courses the school offered. In 1959 she completed a correspondence course in solid geometry with high grades. She expects to study calculus by correspondence after she passes the solid geometry Regents. Attendance at a rural school has not quenched her ambition to become an electronics engineer.

At Grand Gorge, two students recently completed courses in Spanish, a third passed her shorthand examination. A boy whose father operates a television repair business took TV and radio courses, and passed them both. So did his father.

At the Roxbury Central School two students passed correspondence courses in art, one completed a journalism course and entered the School of Journalism at Syracuse University.

A Supervised Correspondence Study Group with representatives from each of the schools in the Catskill Project is now evaluating hundreds of courses and setting up procedures to multiply use of this device with effective safeguards for the students.

Each facet of the Catskill Project is represented by study groups of teachers from the 27 schools. These meet every month in Oneonta. In addition to the correspondence and multiple class groups they include committees on foreign languages, shared services, school aides and flexible scheduling.

If the project did nothing but bring rural teachers together it would perform a valuable service for often they become as isolated as their communities. As a result of these meetings French teachers Margaret Coons of Margaretville and Paul Penrose of Downsville will be able to transmit their enthusiasm to language teachers from the other Catskill schools.

Last summer they attended the language institute at Colgate University where they were introduced to new techniques of teaching beginning French.

"We learn our own language by imitating the sounds we hear at home," Miss Coons explains. "Mastering a modern language is different than mastering a classical language. At the start children need more opportunity to speak, listen, understand and answer back. In the past we've concentrated too much on grammatical analysis which should come later."

Visitors to Miss Coons' French I class, less than a week after the opening of school, are treated to an extraordinary exhibition. In accordance with the principle of oral and aural learning, her students have not as yet seen French words on the blackboard or in their textbooks.

"Bonjour, monsieur," says Miss Coons to the boy in the front row. "Comment vous appelez-vous?"

"Je m'appelle Marcelle," he replies easily.

"Et comment s'appelle-t-elle?" asks the teacher pointing to the girl in the next seat.

"C'est Suzanne," he answers.

After each pupil has identified himself, greeted his

neighbor and inquired of his health and happiness, the class moves into new conversational areas.

The following is a translation of one of a series of dialogs in which every member of the class participates five days after first being exposed to a new language.

"Good morning, John. How are you?"

"Very well, thank you. And you?"

"Not bad, thanks. Who is that?"

"He's a friend."

"What is his name?"

"Paul. Let me introduce you to him. Paul, I'd like you to meet John LeBlanc."

"Hello John, my name is Paul Martin."

"Hello Paul, where are you going?"

"To French class."

"Ah! You're studying French. We too."

"Good, let's go!"

The accents are remarkably free of Catskill intonation but the most surprising feature of the dialogs is the free, uninhibited fluency displayed by most of the class.

Later in the period Miss Coons, not content merely with her pupils' understanding of her own carefully phrased diction, turns on a tape recording of a similar conversation between three Frenchmen. Following the rapid fire dialog there are gaps in the tape for class participation. The class fills in the blanks easily.

"That Colgate experience was most stimulating," says Miss Coons with a proud look toward her class. "Eventually these boys and girls will feel quite at ease in Paris."

Although Margaretville Central School has never offered a fourth year of French it registered another rural break-through this year. Evelyn Fairbairn, the same girl who awakens at 6:30 a.m. on Saturday for the "able and ambitious" program in Oneonta, is taking her fourth year course from an extremely articulate tape recorder.

"Evelyn has mastered her grammar," explains Miss Coons. "Her problem is pronunciation. My problem is availability to teach her. So she learns correct pronunciation from tapes made by Frenchmen. There are blank places on the tape where she can do her own recording. I can then check her diction and make my own corrections on the same tape. At her next session she can listen to the playback and go on from there. In addition, she is reading French literature and her comments on tape will give me further insight into both her understanding and handling of the language."

This year Miss Coons and Mr. Penrose will compare their language experiences with other Catskill teachers at 15 meetings organized by the project. Expanded use of tape recorders and multiple classes will play an important part in the discussions.

The U.S. Office of Education reports that only one in seven high school students studies a modern foreign language, a shocking indictment of our ineptitude in a shrunken world. The Catskill Project demonstrates that rural schools are capable of overcoming any inherent deficiencies.

At Hancock Central School Miss Lent teaches two French classes simultaneously; in South Kortright bright students begin foreign languages in the seventh grade, take more advanced work as high school freshmen. Grand Gorge, undismayed by a total high school enrollment of 55, has a similar program.

Edward A. Burke, supervising principal of South Kortright for the past 30 years, is a creative member of the project's Executive Committee. He has a twinkle in his eyes as he explains his philosophy of change: "Some fellows hang around waiting to retire and don't want to try anything new. The only way I can stay young is to keep experimenting. I want you to know that I'm proud of people like our French teacher of the past 30 years who refused to get into a rut and shifted over to that new conversational method of teaching. She thinks it's great and I think *she's* great."

This ability to accept change enables the librarian at Margaretville to share her dignified precincts with a jukebox. It is precisely like a rock 'n' roll jukebox with one exception—the records are conversational French and students can plug earphones into eight positions in the cabinet and listen to the dialog without disturbing their neighbors.

Dr. Cyr regards this jukebox as a symbol of mechanical enlightenment, the precursor of technological advance in education.

"One day, and it isn't very far away, we'll be able to select appropriate tape, TV and film segments as easily as we press the button on the jukebox," he predicts. "The problem is to get the right material at the time you need it and we're working on that now."

Included in the right material for a rural community without a physics teacher is a high school physics course on film prepared by University of California Professor Harvey White. Filmed in 162 half-hour lessons in color and black-and-white, it is sold to schools by Encyclopaedia Films, Inc. The grant from the Fund for the Advancement of Education has provided a print which is circulated among the Catskill schools.

Increased use of such resources is on the docket for the future. A program in which teacher specialists are shared exists now.

"Our school is too small to afford a full-time psychologist, a dental hygienist or a teacher for youngsters with special learning problems," says Supervising Principal Elton F. S. Shaver of Margaretville. "Other schools in the Catskill Project lack nurses, guidance counselors, remedial reading experts and teachers of industrial arts and agriculture. New York State has an excellent program which enables two or more schools to share these specialists.

"The psychologist visits us 40 days a year and his circuit includes five other schools; we share a dental hygienist with two schools and send youngsters who require special classes to Arkville. We've got a ninth grade shop teacher so the boys from the Fleischmanns School who don't have one, drive over for that period. The cooperating communities split the expenses and New York reimburses us substantially under the State aid program. In the old days we had circuit-riding preachers, now we've got circuit-riding teachers."

Although these programs existed in New York long before the Catskill Project, a Study Group on Shared Services representing the 27 schools is considering an enlargement of the idea to include scientific and technological equipment which would otherwise be too expensive for them individually.

The high promise of the Catskill Project is reflected by the willingness of the communities to absorb costs which were initially paid by the Fund for the Advancement of Education. Local schools now transport and feed the teacher study groups which trade experiences at Oneonta each month and the Margaretville Board of Education has approved the expenditure of $30 for each youngster attending the "able and ambitious" seminars. In 1959, Catskill Project members agreed voluntarily to pay $25,000 of the $37,000 in salaries to school aides formerly charged to the Fund.

The aides, who are paid approximately $1.70 an hour, are vital to the project.

"You need more time to prepare for multiple classes," says mathematics teacher Matalavage, "and aides who relieve you of routine clerical chores, give you that time."

Last year his aide was a Margaretville mother. She mimeographed quizzes, handled correspondence, typed learner's guides and corrected objective tests for Matalavage and three other teachers. In addition, she assisted the librarian in processing new books and keeping the card catalog up-to-date. As part of the enrichment program stimulated by the project she prepared bibliographies for students working on special reports. The aides, carefully selected, mature women, perform no teaching functions. They simply free teachers to do the jobs for which they were trained.

Aides are utilized in varying ways by Catskill Project schools. At South Otselic Central School an aide working a 5-hour-day handles orders for films, corrects objective portions of tests, distributes project materials to the faculty, acts as part-time secretary to the guidance counselor, files materials for the agriculture class and types menus for the cafeteria.

In Delhi, Mrs. Jean Dreyfus, widow of a lawyer and mother of three, supervises study halls, freeing a teacher from an unprofitable hour. In addition to keeping the peace during the period, Mrs. Dreyfus serves the faculty by indexing materials, scoring mechanical examinations and filing achievement tests for the guidance counselor.

At Schenevus the savings stamp program with all its clerical detail is supervised by an aide instead of a harassed teacher. In other schools aides take attendance, handle correspondence to parents, monitor cafeterias and playgrounds, obtain films and set up film projectors, order supplies and generally make themselves useful in hundreds of small but vital ways.

Most Catskill teachers and administrators agree that school aides are an investment in economy since they perform the same *nonprofessional* chores as teachers at a lower salary.

An enthusiastic booster of the school aide program is Ivan Miller, Margaretville's guidance counselor. He has had many clerical burdens lifted by the aides, enabling him to work more intensively with his students. In line with project philosophy that the small school is unique and should not imitate its larger counterparts, he has developed a system of flexible scheduling.

"In the past, classes met daily for 40 minutes," he reports, "but now they meet four times a week for an hour. In the process we've gained much more than the 40 minutes of total class time during the week. We find that longer periods lend themselves to multiple class teaching and to better preparation for the next day's work. The fact that students don't have the same classes at the same time each day seems to be stimulating too. At least," he adds with a smile, "they spread their fatigue equally among the teachers."

With guidance counselors from the other Catskill

schools, Miller attends a flexible scheduling study group at Oneonta which seeks to refine small school programming. He and his colleagues regard the teacher's detailed knowledge of a youngster as a distinct advantage of the rural school.

"A child's strongest recollection of school usually concerns the individual help he received," he says. "All learning has to be individual and here we know the youngster and his background intimately."

A husky junior who transferred to Margaretville from a large New York City high school, seconds the motion.

"Here the teachers seem to understand you better," he says, "and I think I understand them better. I know kids above and below my class but when I was in New York I just knew the fellows in my own class. I never even got to meet the principal. His door was always closed—unless you got into terrible trouble or belonged to the Student Council. Mr. Shaver's door is always open."

Principal Shaver, known affectionately to his students as "Prof," has an open mind as well as an open door.

"A rural school is very much a family situation," he says. "We're much closer to the parents. After all, we meet them on the street every day. But this is not enough. There is no such thing as an adequate school whether rural or urban. You've got to have vision and realize continually that more can be done. The Catskill Project gives form to this vision. Project people meet with our board of education, keep the PTA informed and work with our staff. It's important to realize that teachers are not forced to work with the project. We have some very able people who prefer to work out their own patterns and we try to avoid pressuring them."

The teachers outside the project as well as those within

are aware that many problems are still to be ironed out. Multiple class teaching is not yet an unqualified success. Teachers report that large classes are difficult to manage, and there are indications that slow learners cannot keep up as well in a room divided into several groups. It may be necessary to introduce more self-direction in elementary education to prepare the high schoolers to assume a greater share of responsibility. As with any experiment, there are teachers temperamentally unable to accept new procedures. As "Prof" Shaver pointed out, these include some gifted teachers. One of them is Marian Connell, who teaches physics and mathematics at Margaretville.

"I'm just enough of a New England Yankee to like to think for myself," she explains. "I don't feel the need of multiple classes in my subject and I certainly don't need physics films. I majored in physics and I'm perfectly capable of teaching it. When the project people come back from those meetings in Oneonta they act as though they've found the Grail. I don't think they have."

Miss Connell is regarded by her colleagues as a teacher of exceptional ability who experiments constantly to stimulate her pupils. She has set up "free labs" where talented students work out problems springing from their own scientific interests and half her physics students are girls, a percentage rarely matched in city schools. Ultimately the Catskill Project hopes to enlist her talents in its cause.

Historically the project sprang from earlier efforts to pool knowledge about schools in the Delaware-Otsego-Chenango County area. The Catskill Area Study Council which had met at the State University College of Education at Oneonta and the New York Central School Study with offices at Teachers College, Columbia University, joined forces for cooperative research in the spring of 1954.

Schoolmen credit Dr. Cyr with breathing life into the group. Chairman of the Columbia University Seminar on Rural Life and former president of the National Education Association's Department of Rural Education, he has spent the past 35 years working to improve small schools. He helped to coordinate the proposals submitted to the Fund for the Advancement of Education. The Fund's $120,000 grant in March 1957 put the Catskill Project in motion and a later grant of $110,000 has helped to bring it to its present status.

The contribution of the State University College of Education at Oneonta has been indispensable to the project. Among other things it has donated space for project headquarters.

Dr. Royal F. Netzer, its president, says, "We're interested in the constant revision of our curriculum in preparing teachers for small schools. By cooperating closely with the Catskill Project we can make our own program more effective."

Dr. Netzer was one of the originators of the Saturday programs for the "able and ambitious."

"I think," he reflects, "that it has raised the level of aspiration of these youngsters and their parents. This year, in addition to the mathematics and science programs, we're having two classes in the humanities."

Evelyn Fairbairn of Margaretville High School is one of the humanities students. When the alarm clock rings at 6:30 these Saturday mornings she prepares for college level work in creative writing, literature, music and visual arts. In her case, as well as in many others, the Catskill Project has produced an unexpected by-product.

"As a result of these meetings," she says, "I've decided to major in mathematics at college and then I hope to become a teacher."

"Prof" Shaver and his faculty agree that she'll be a good one.

For further information on the Catskill Area Project contact:

Noble J. Gividen, Coordinator
Catskill Area Project
215 Home Economics Building
State University College of Education
Oneonta, N.Y.

For related experimental programs see Appendix, pp. 187–89.

8. The Electronic Link:

TELEVISION IN SOUTHWESTERN INDIANA

Television's role in spanning rural school systems is being explored by the Southwestern Indiana Educational Television Council. New patterns of cooperation between separate school districts and between educational and commercial television have been established. The result is an economical use of television which promises rich educational rewards.

SOUTH TERRACE ELEMENTARY
School, which is surrounded by cornfields, draws its students from the townships of Griffin, Cynthiana, Poseyville and Wadesville, Ind. Two years ago there was no science program for these children. Today any fifth grade boy or girl can describe and diagram a jet engine or a rocket. Two years ago there were no foreign languages taught in the elementary schools of the area. Today conversational Spanish is spoken by every third and fourth grader.

The Southwestern Indiana Educational Television Council is responsible for this ferment. The council links 24 separate school corporations and transmits lessons to more than 23,000 youngsters in 108 schools within a 60-mile radius of Evansville.

The televised lessons are similar in quality and technique to those of Washington County, Md. (see chapter 5) but the council has pioneered in new patterns of organization and economy. It has pooled the resources of many school systems and avoided huge capital outlays by renting the facilities of a commercial television station. Today it enrolls additional schools at the modest cost of $4 a pupil.

Evansville Superintendent Ralph Becker and his colleagues of the Southwestern Indiana Superintendent's Association are responsible for these innovations.

Becker's interest had been stimulated in 1957 by the work of Dr. Alexander J. Stoddard. Dr. Stoddard, a former superintendent of schools in Providence, Denver, Philadelphia and Los Angeles, and Schenectady and Bronxville, N.Y., had studied big city educational programs for the Fund for the Advancement of Education. In his report, *Schools for Tomorrow: An Educator's Blueprint,* Dr. Stoddard wrote, "The use of television in the educational program, not only to supplement and enrich, but also to perform certain functions heretofore performed by teachers, and to cover areas of the regular curriculum as an integral part, offers great hope for meeting teacher and building shortages, but more important, for raising the level of teaching."

In conversations with Dr. Stoddard, Superintendent Becker had described the common problems faced by many of the southwestern Indiana school systems. There were great disparities from community to community and the rural schools suffered particularly from the shortage of qualified teachers. Only a limited number of teaching specialists were available to larger cities like Evansville. In the era of outer space, southwestern Indiana lagged in its science programs. Becker wondered whether the 16 corporations represented in the superintendents' association could band together, strengthen curriculum jointly and spread their gifted teachers further by television. Dr. Stoddard encouraged his interest.

There was a myriad of obstacles. The school systems guarded their autonomy with a fierce pride strengthened by rivalry in Indiana's major pastime—basketball. They had polite but distant relationships. The independent farmers who comprised the bulk of the population regarded television as a toy for idle hours, not a tool for mastery of the three R's.

Then there was the scheduling problem. Each community started and ended school at a different time and there was no uniformity in scheduling subject matter. It seemed hopeless.

The trim, white-haired Becker persisted in his explorations. In late 1957 he talked to Richard Shively, manager of television station WTVW, channel 7, Evansville. This affiliate of the American Broadcasting Company had gone on the air in 1956 and its VHF signal covered a 60-mile radius. As a fledgling commercial station its studio and equipment were idle until 2 p.m.

Earlier Shively had offered these facilities during the unused hours to Becker on a nonprofit basis.

When Becker asked if the offer was still open Shively arrived at a charge of $100 a day which would cover the cost of five studio employees, transmitter and camera tubes. The station would pay for power, light and maintenance of the TV cameras.

Things were looking up. Technical facilities were available at a reasonable charge. The superintendents were beginning to accept with enthusiasm the idea that television could play a useful role in improving education. The banding together of school corporations seemed sufficiently unique to assure a foundation grant to help southwestern Indiana over its first financial hurdles.

On February 19, 1958, the superintendents' association formed the Southwestern Indiana Educational Television

Council, consisting of representatives of the 16 school corporations. These districts ranged in size from Evansville's 37,000 students to New Harmony's 337.

Along with the optimism came rumbles of discontent from some school trustees and principals. The objections they raised could be answered only by Dr. Stoddard, who had observed televised classes all over the United States.

On March 31 Stoddard, whose unflagging energy and creativeness belied his 69 years, steamed into Evansville to present the case for television to a joint meeting of the superintendents and their boards of school trustees.

Becker recalls the Stoddard eloquence. "That man can be talking and you can tell yourself, 'I'm agin' it, I'm agin' it' but pretty soon you're not agin' it."

Stoddard was so persuasive that the school trustees of Boonville held a meeting immediately after his talk and agreed to subscribe to the televised lessons.

But how could school corporations disburse funds to the council? There was no law permitting this sort of thing.

"You can't do it," said a member of the State Board of Accounts, "it's never been done before."

Becker and his associates now became politicians and set machinery in motion for the eventual passage of a bill in the Indiana Senate. Although televised instruction began in September 1958, the legislation was not passed until March 1959. Fortunately it was worded, "A bill for an act to authorize school corporations to join together to conduct educational television instruction and to legalize expenditures *previously* made for such purposes."

Having launched this legislation the council now wangled approval from the State Department of Public Instruction and Indiana's General Commission of Education for televised lessons.

The council hired a small staff directed by Glen H. Traw, for 40 years a teacher, principal, superintendent and athletic coach in the area. As his production director Mr. Traw selected Robert Edelman, an English teacher from Evansville's Bosse High School who had had radio and television experience. Everett Lenon, for 52 years an Indiana teacher and principal, was placed in charge of evaluating the effectiveness of the televised lessons. A part-time artist to create visuals and several secretaries rounded out the staff. Offices were set up in an abandoned old school adjacent to WTVW.

The Ford Foundation granted the council $75,000 for the first year of its operation after which the amounts were to be reduced annually to $60,000, $30,000 and zero. The council estimated its expenditures for the first year to be $150,000. The $75,000 it lacked was made up by charges of $500 apiece to participating school systems plus an assessment based on their pupil population. These amounts ranged from the $37,618 paid by Evansville to New Harmony's $1,036.

On March 31, 1958, less than 4 weeks after Dr. Stoddard's appearance, principals of the participating schools met with the council to arrange a television schedule for the following September.

What had seemed an "insurmountable" problem was soon overcome.

Children would receive no more than one of the six 25-minute television lessons a day. There would be 15-minute classroom followups in elementary school and 30-minute followups in high school.

As cautious as this seemed, some school corporations insisted on additional safeguards. The Vincennes and Washington schools added a clause to the contract permitting them to withdraw if "nonessential curricular offerings are made a part of the project, to wit, conversational foreign languages, or the like."

A year later, Vincennes and Washington would participate in the seventh and most popular TV course, conversational Spanish.

In May of 1958 auditions were held for the selection of six studio teachers. More than 20 teachers competed, televising sample lessons. The quality of their presentations convinced the selection committee that talent need never be imported.

During the summer of 1958 a four-week workshop joined studio teachers, classroom teachers who would receive their telecasts, principals of the participating schools and supervisors of the subject matter to be taught. Here the content of the television courses was hammered out. In fifth, sixth, seventh and eighth grade science, where no unified curriculum had existed, modern developments were incorporated into an exciting framework. In ninth grade English, eleventh grade United States history, twelfth grade government and tenth grade geometry the exchange of ideas produced strengthened courses.

On September 3, 1958, at 8:30 a.m., an English teacher named Joyce Warrick inaugurated educational television in southwestern Indiana. During that first year 11,803 students received part of their education by television.

Graphic evidence of the success of the first year of the experiment was provided by enrollments for the 1959–60 school year. The number of students doubled. Schools in

Daviess County, Ky.; 3 Illinois communities; 3 Indiana districts, and 4 Catholic schools of the Evansville Diocese joined the original 16 corporations. The $4.21 cost per TV pupil of the first year made it economically feasible to accept new students for $4 apiece. Though the foundation grant was reduced by $15,000 the course in conversational Spanish was added.

Now the schedule read:

PROGRAM NO.	TIME—A.M.	GRADE LEVEL	PROGRAM (DAILY, MON.—FRI.)
1	8:30–8:55	9	First semester: English I (literature) Second semester: English II (grammar)
2	9:00–9:25	5–6	Science—health—safety
3	9:30–9:55	11	U.S. History I and II
4	10:05–10:30	7–8	Science—health—safety
5	10:30–10:55	12	First semester: government Second semester: economics and sociology
6	11:00–11:15	3–4	Conversational Spanish
7	11:30–11:55	10	Geometry I and II

Parents at home could tune to their children's classes on channel 7. They developed a new appreciation for the quality of teaching as they saw at first hand the dramatic possibilities of educational television. The mayor of Evansville was sworn in during a government telecast. Geometry students watched a demonstration of the electrocardiograph and were shown how its reading depends upon the Pythagorean theorem. A mock trial conducted by a local lawyer revealed the techniques of justice more vividly than a textbook. An Air Force pilot described the mechanics of his jet plane and the problems of penetrating outer space. Headlines came alive as he explained to intermediate science students the features of the "moonsuit" to be worn by the astronauts.

Letters poured into the studio. Mrs. Hamman, the Spanish teacher, received her share.

A lady from New Harmony wrote, "I appreciate being able to join the third and fourth graders via television for the conversational Spanish classes. I have started night classes to learn Spanish, thanks to you for getting me interested. I think you are doing an excellent job, both for school children and quite a few housewives."

One writer summed up her reaction to Spanish simply, "I enjoy it more than any other program on television."

A beautician described her morning routine.

"I simply turn to Channel 7 at 11 in my beauty shop and keep my fingers crossed I can get all the new words."

Rev. James R. Deneen, superintendent of schools of the Evansville Diocese, discussed the cooperation between public and parochial schools.

"Our teachers are notably deficient in elementary science," he said. "The $4 a year cost per child makes our participation financially feasible. Our youngsters and our PTA's are most enthusiastic."

Like the Catholic schools, the rural public schools had suffered from a deficiency of science teaching.

Bill Wilson, whose South Terrace Elementary School replaced four one-room schools, agrees with Father Deneen.

"Our women teachers have not learned science in an organized, systematic way. Since the start of televised lessons, teachers and students have lost their fear of science."

Seventy South Terrace fifth and sixth graders view the telecasts in a large room after which their classroom teacher conducts imaginative followup sessions. These include panel discussions of such subjects as steam engines, gas turbines and rocketry. At a recent class meeting an argument about the peacetime uses of atomic energy was settled by a pigtailer who had done some outside reading on the medical applications of radioisotopes.

Evansville high school teachers point out that elementary science has been lifted to the secondary level and they are now busy raising their own sights.

Large-class viewing has resulted in better utilization of teachers.

At Dexter School in Evansville, one qualified science teacher oversees 170 seventh and eighth graders in one television classroom and 225 fifth and sixth graders in another. A secretary handles all his paperwork. In 2 periods he teaches as many students as were taught in 12 conventional classes. The quality of the students' science notebooks attests to the ability of large classes to concentrate on well-presented material.

Large classes have freed teachers for critically needed counseling services and for the development of new courses. A small class in advanced chemistry and biology for gifted students at Bosse High School was made possible by the release of a qualified teacher from a conventional assignment now handled by television.

Mrs. Anne Massengill, the young adult librarian at the Evansville Public Library, reports another impact of television.

"There has been a marked increase in the use of the

library. A month ago, for example, the ninth grade English TV teacher discussed American myths and legends. The subject had been covered before television but we had seen little effect in the library. This time we were swamped. From original interest in American mythology the children switched to the legends of other countries. Until this fall those books sat on our shelves, now they are being read.

"We can't buy enough science books," she continues, "and for the first time we are getting requests for books relating to projects in mathematics.

"When Mr. Wiggers, the TV history teacher, recommends a book about Lincoln or Jackson and asks students to let him know their reactions we're sure to be deluged. There is no doubt in my mind that television is raising educational standards in Evansville."

As in Washington County, Md., the studio teachers are responsible for only one class a day. This enables them to prepare lessons of uniformly high quality. Some average 12 hours of preparation every day with extra work on weekends. They are paid the same salaries as classroom teachers.

When Joyce Warrick lectured on *Great Expectations* she wore a Victorian costume and read from the 1856 issue of Harper's, in which the story was published. The authentic writing desk, daguerreotypes and foot warmer on the set enhanced the mood as the teacher related the book to the architecture, apparel and social conflict of the period.

Local industrial and cultural groups have enriched television teaching. Expensive scientific equipment is made available by many firms, the zoo lends it animals, the museum its artifacts and retail stores are generous with their products.

Close links are maintained between studio and classroom teachers. Seminars in November, February and May enable them to evaluate and improve the courses. Over 300 teachers attended the last meeting. At the May seminar study guides for the television classes are reviewed and revised. Feedback cards from the classroom to the studio teachers keep the latter informed continuously about the strengths and weaknesses of their presentation.

At the time of this writing less than two years of the three-year experiment have been completed and the Southwestern Indiana Education Television Council, though delighted with results, is unwilling to make claims based on achievement tests to date.

At the end of the first year, however, it summarized its comparisons of television and nontelevision students of the same mental caliber:

"Students tested from grades 5 to 12 in the television-help taught classes seem to learn as much as, and in some cases significantly more than, comparable students taught in the conventional classes. These comparisons were taken from some 30 groups in 6 different areas of instruction and involved more than 14,000 students in the 10 counties of southwestern Indiana."

The council's evaluators, whose work has been verified by the Indiana University Bureau of Measurement, further concluded that "The scores of the TV-help taught classes ranked better than the national established norms in most cases."

Pupils have been asked their opinion of television in unsigned questionnaires. Here are the responses of 3,000 intermediate science students.

	YES %	NO %
Do you like TV lessons in science?	86.3	13.7
Does teaching by TV make science easier to learn?	80.4	19.6
Do you learn more from TV lessons?	81.8	18.2
Do drawings and experiments help you to learn?	94.2	5.8
Have you learned to take notes better?	92.2	7.8
Have you learned to pay better attention?	89.0	11.0
Would you like more time for class discussion?	55.3	44.7
Do you think the class is too large?	31.4	68.6
Do you understand the material in the TV lessons?	83.4	16.6
Does science on TV make you want to learn more science?	74.9	25.1
Would you like to continue science by TV next year?	79.6	20.4

In all courses, with the exception of English, student opinion favored the use of television overwhelmingly. In English only 47.6 percent of the students said they liked the TV class. Perhaps an explanation for this attitude is found in their answer to the question "Is too much expected of you?" To this, 60 percent answered in the affirmative. In spite of this, more than half the English students said that television offered them a better opportunity for learning, 86.1 percent replied that it offered good training in note-taking and outlining and 67.1 percent said they considered the studio teacher as much one of their teachers as the classroom teacher.

The Indiana experiment is part of The National Program in the Use of Television in the Public Schools, a project supported by grants from the Ford Foundation and the Fund for the Advancement of Education. This program was an outgrowth of Dr. Stoddard's report. Now in its third year it involves 178,000 television students in 775 schools in over 250 school systems in 15 States.

At the end of the first year of the National Program achievement tests were taken by 14,326 television students and 12,666 non-TV students of equal ability. In 38 comparisons of these groups there were statistically significant differences in achievement—29 favored the television classes, 9 the control students.

A report on the second year of the National Program is now available from the Fund for the Advancement of Education as is the publication *Teaching by Television* which ranges beyond the boundaries of the National Program.

In Evansville the pioneers of the southwest Indiana experiment believe they have found a down-to-earth method of utilizing television. Dick Shively, WTVW's manager, believes that there are many television stations willing to cooperate with the schools. At a time when commercial television is being forced to turn more of its energies to public service, this hope may become a reality.

Meanwhile Superintendent Becker and his colleagues are looking forward to an expansion of their television activities. They expect thousands of new students to enroll at $4 apiece, and they envision their council on a self-supporting basis when the foundation grants expire.

"Television has succeeded beyond our expectations,"

states Becker, "in the quality of courses taught, in the enthusiastic acceptance by communities it has touched and by the self-improvement it has stimulated."

The boys and girls from Cynthiana, Poseyville and Wadesville have a lot to look forward to. These rural youngsters have advantages denied to millions of children in the major cities of America. The television receivers in their Indiana classrooms are windows on the world.

> For further information about Indiana television contact:
>
>> Glen H. Traw, Director
>> Southwestern Indiana Educational
>>   Television Council
>> 425 Carpenter St.
>> Evansville, Ind.
>
> For copies of Dr. Stoddard's report *Schools for Tomorrow;* and for copies of *The National Program in the Use of Television in the Public Schools: A Report on the Second Year;* and *Teaching by Television* contact:
>
>> Fund for the Advancement of Education
>> 477 Madison Ave.
>> New York 22, N.Y.
>
> For related experimental programs see Appendix, pp. 179–80.

9. Teachers of Tomorrow:

THE HARVARD PROGRAM

Where do we find the teachers of tomorrow? Once we have recruited them, how do we retain them? How does education meet the competition of professions offering greater salaries and greater prestige?

In the face of these crushing problems there have been wails of anguish from teachers and, understandably, they have concentrated on salary betterment as the solution.

Perhaps the solution is more complex, involving new methods of recruitment, new approaches to teacher training and new roles for the teacher. Hopeful progress in these directions has been made by programs centered at Harvard University.

IN MANY RESPECTS TEACHERS BELONG
to a second-class profession. They have been grossly underpaid. Their ranks have attracted less than the best college graduates; in fact about 25 percent of U.S. elementary school teachers are *not* college graduates.

The competition that characterizes industry's search for talented undergraduates is lacking in the field of education. Everyone seeks the brilliant physicist of tomorrow. Who seeks the brilliant teacher?

University faculties of arts and science display little respect for training programs in teachers colleges and schools of education. In the acknowledged "conflict" between liberal arts and education the latter has been downgraded intellectually.

In contrast to other professions teaching makes little provision for the advancement of its most gifted specialists. Its appeal, particularly to men, has been limited sharply by the absence of clear-cut career patterns.

Salary questions have dominated the hue and cry about the teacher shortage but there has been little public focus on the absence of prestige, fulfillment, advancement and recognition in the profession. Debates about the shortage in quantity and quality have overlooked the untapped reservoirs of teaching talent.

These problems have been tackled simultaneously and imaginatively by Harvard's Graduate School of Education, the Harvard Faculty of Arts and Sciences and the Radcliffe Graduate School. Results in recruiting and holding teachers of superior ability are so encouraging that colleges and universities throughout the United States are planning to emulate the Harvard program.

In 1952 Harvard joined forces with eastern liberal arts colleges to form the Twenty-Nine College Cooperative Plan.* Purpose of the plan—to stimulate outstanding liberal arts graduates to enter the teaching profession.

The year before the plan was instituted there were only 50 students enrolled in the Graduate School's Master of Arts in Teaching Program. In 1959–60 there are 231 M.A.T. students preparing for high school teaching during a "fifth year" at Harvard. An additional 62 are working toward a master of education degree for elementary school teaching.

In the seven years since the formation of the Twenty-Nine College Plan, Harvard has trained 1,259 teachers, 766 of whom came from the cooperating colleges. During that period applications from the 29 colleges have tripled. The Graduate School of Education, which had once faced the problem of a scarcity of students, has a new dilemma—

---

* The colleges are Amherst, Barnard, Bates, Bennington, Bowdoin, Brown, Bryn Mawr, Colby, Colgate, Connecticut, Dartmouth, Hamilton, Harvard, Haverford, Holy Cross, Lafayette, Massachusetts Institute of Technology, Middlebury, Mount Holyoke, Pembroke, Radcliffe, Sarah Lawrence, Simmons, Smith, Swarthmore, Vassar, Wellesley, Wheaton, and Williams.

it receives more applications from qualified candidates than it can accept.

This successful recruiting record stems partly from the activity at each of the 29 colleges of one of its faculty members acting as a representative of the program. He provides information about the fifth year of graduate training at Harvard and stimulates student interest. Visits to each campus by members of the Harvard staff and joint meetings of the college representatives maintain continuing awareness of the program.

Liberal arts graduates accepted in the internship programs begin their training in the Harvard-Newton Summer School. They receive an immediate baptism of fire, teaching elementary, junior and senior high school classes under the supervision of master teachers and Harvard faculty members. During the seven-week session in 1959 they taught over 900 students attending the three Newton schools utilized for this purpose. Their pupils are drawn from 10 cooperating school systems in the area. Elementary and junior high pupils represent a cross section of the school population. Senior high school students, selected on the basis of outstanding ability, receive credit for their work.

The Harvard trainees teach and observe in the morning. During the afternoon they confer with master teachers and Harvard faculty who help to plan and evaluate their teaching. In addition, they take courses in curriculum and methods.

"I almost died!" exclaims Carol Armstrong, a Mount Holyoke graduate, recalling the intensive summer schedule. "But once I got over the shock, a whole new world opened up."

Elizabeth Frothingam, who earned highest honors in English literature at Principia College, reflects majority opinion about the exposure to the classroom *before* studying teaching methods.

"You do a lot of unraveling when you stand in front of a class and come face-to-face with practical problems. When you study teaching techniques later you are better able to relate the information to your classroom experience. You haven't started out in a predetermined mold. I think it helps you to remain more of an individual."

Following the Harvard-Newton Summer Program the candidates for graduate degrees spend half the academic year as full-time graduate students and the remaining half as intern teachers in nearby school systems.

As graduate students they further the Harvard contention that expertness in subject matter is essential to successful teaching. Faculties of education and of arts and sciences have joined forces and the M.A.T. Administrative Board consists of representatives from both faculties.

Each student has two advisers—one in his specialized subject drawn from arts and sciences, one in the overall field chosen from education.

As Harvard's Official Register puts it, "The requirements allow the student to pursue his own intellectual interests and each student is encouraged to make maximum use of the resources of the entire university."

During their half-year on campus most master of arts in teaching candidates take three or more half courses under the faculty of arts and sciences. Prospective high school history teachers study with historians like Arthur Schlesinger, Jr., and Oscar Handlin. Future English teachers take classes with such eminent professors as Archibald

MacLeish and Howard Mumford Jones. During the past 10 years the number of arts and sciences courses taken by students in the Graduate School of Education has increased from 56 to 586.

In addition to courses in his subject field the Harvard trainee selects three half courses basic to education. These include educational psychology and measurement, philosophy or history of education, and the sociology of education. The program is rounded out with a half course in the curriculum and methods of teaching in the student's subject field.

These requirements vary depending upon the trainee's undergraduate experience. If education courses had been woven into his liberal arts program or if he passes appraisal examinations in these subjects he is not required to take them in graduate school. Some candidates for the master of arts in teaching have taken as much as three-quarters of their work in arts and sciences.

Future elementary and secondary teachers receive full course credit for their half-year of intern teaching. The internship program is a striking innovation pioneered by Harvard and its public school partners.

Teachers, supervisors and principals of 10 cooperating school systems work with the Graduate School of Education in assisting the interns. This is one of the links in improved university-public school relationships as described by Dean Keppel on page 20.

Interns receive $1,800 for their half-year of teaching. Their salaries are paid by the local school systems. In many cases this sum makes their graduate training possible. Internship helps to solve the economic problems plaguing a would-be "master teacher" torn between the desire for graduate work and the need to earn a livelihood. It presents new alternatives to assistance by foundations such as the Fund for the Advancement of Education and the Ford Foundation whose grants have made the program possible.

Added incentive is given by several of the school systems which offer a year of teaching credit on the salary schedules of former interns hired as full-fledged teachers.

The interns are of extraordinary caliber. Most of them admit that they were attracted by the superior quality of the Harvard program and appalled by the prospect of conventional teacher training.

Howard Johnson is a former Phi Beta Kappa mathematics major from the University of Kansas. As an intern plane geometry teacher at Newton High School his competence was recognized immediately. His occasional assignments to teach the Advanced Placement class in calculus have added zest to his teaching ambitions.

How many high school history teachers will have Nancy Stein's qualifications? She majored in history at Radcliffe, graduating cum laude. A specialist in 20th century United States diplomatic history, she is an intern teacher at Newton High School. Among other classes she has been assigned two of the top history groups for whom she has helped to develop an enriched program.

"My Harvard experience has been grueling but stimulating," she says, "and I have been delighted by the summer school and by the education courses."

Following her internship she is scheduled to take four additional history courses at Harvard, one given by a professor whom she regards as the foremost colonial historian.

The eagerness of schools to hire former interns is the

most eloquent testimonial to their ability. The Newton Public Schools have long been regarded as one of the Nation's outstanding systems. Last year 30 interns taught in Newton—20 were invited to join the system.

"The Harvard interns have been exceptionally promising," says Dr. Charles E. Brown, Newton's assistant superintendent. "When compared to the total group available for new teaching positions the interns tend to be intellectually superior. In addition, they are well rounded and accomplished in fields outside their teaching specialty. These people would be successful in any field. They enter this profession because they sincerely want to teach."

W. Eugene Ferguson, who heads the mathematics department at Newton High School, adds, "Their commitment to teaching becomes apparent immediately. Their own intellectual standard is high, they expect more of their students and they transmit this attitude to the class."

Past studies of men and women entering the teaching profession have tended to indicate that they were of lower caliber intellectually than those entering other professions. The Harvard group reverses this impression.

Students entering the Graduate School of Education from Harvard College won proportionately more honors as undergraduates than had classmates entering 60 medical schools.

More than that, they have remained in the teaching profession.

Judson T. Shaplin, associate dean of the Harvard Graduate School of Education, has analyzed a followup study of 692 graduates of the M.A.T. program from 1947 to 1957.

Dr. Shaplin found that 89 percent of the men and 93 percent of the women entered classroom teaching after graduation. After 10 years 71 percent of the men and 57 percent of the women were still employed full time in educational institutions. Many of those not so employed are advanced students or members of the Armed Forces. Thirty-seven percent of the men and 73 percent of the women in this group stated that they would definitely or probably return to teaching.

The average salary for men after 9 or 10 years of teaching was $6,300, for women $5,500. Thirty percent of the men earned more than $7,000.

"Particularly satisfying," writes Dr. Shaplin, "is the fact that of those still employed in educational institutions, 86 percent of the men and 82 percent of the women declare they are satisfied with their present positions, even though 58 percent of the men and 27 percent of the women find it necessary to supplement their incomes with part-time or summer employment."

In its programs the Graduate School of Education is working toward the development of new career patterns which, while improving education, will lead to greater rewards in salary and prestige for high caliber teachers. New teacher roles, as in team teaching at the Franklin School of Lexington, Mass. (see chapter 1), call for men and women of superior ability.

The Boston area is a center of school experimentation. In addition to the 10 school districts maintaining internship arrangements with Harvard, more than 20 districts take part in the Graduate School of Education's apprenticeship plan also leading to the degrees of master of education and master of arts in teaching.

The apprenticeship plan is more conventional than the internship program and does not include the Harvard-

Newton Summer School or paid intern teaching. The first half of the year is spent in full-time course work. The second half consists of apprentice teaching in the cooperating school districts and additional course work. The standards are equally high and students are of comparable quality.

Dean Francis Keppel of the Graduate School of Education, says, "Nothing of a permanent character can be accomplished for the improvement of the schools without giving first attention to the quality of the staff."

One of the characteristics of teacher education at Harvard is its fostering of questioning attitudes on the part of students. There is a conscious attack on educational dogma and a continuing appeal to the inquiring mind.

"We hold that there is no sacrosanct methodology," says a faculty member. "Here the high priests of the temple are nonexistent."

As one student wrote, "One thing I've found here at Harvard is the attitude that one should question the validity of everything you read. My training had been one of accepting pretty much what you have read and are told. Harvard comes as sort of a shock but I think it is a good thing."

A Committee on Teaching of the Harvard Faculty of Arts and Sciences was appointed by President Pusey to stimulate student interest in teaching as a career. In 1957 they reported grimly about the status of American teachers:

"They live on the fringes of the middle class. But they cannot afford to indulge in the tastes of their peers. Neither can they revolt like the 'bohemian,' since the community demands of them an utter respectability. They can only withdraw timidly to a self-contained world of their own, with its own standards, often entirely out of touch with reality. They—and their wives and children—make admirable sacrifices. But in doing so, they confirm society's impressions of a lowly group, not quite first class and deserving of no better than the hand-me-downs of our civilization. For many young men, therefore, the choice of teaching as a career seems to demand a rejection of the dominant values of their society. To make the break calls for a high degree of motivation and dedication on the part of people who have alternatives open to them. The danger is that the profession may come to accept those without alternatives, literally those good for nothing else."

This picture is being brightened by widespread experimentation. Now 14 additional colleges have joined the original 29 affiliated with Harvard. Harvard's recruitment and internship programs are being adopted by other universities in regional arrangements with liberal arts colleges. Grants from the Ford Foundation have made possible "breakthrough" programs in teacher education on an unprecedented scale. Among the recipients have been Barnard College, Bucknell University, Brown University, Central Michigan University, University of Chicago, Claremont Graduate School, Cornell University, Duke University, George Peabody College for Teachers, Johns Hopkins University, Michigan State University, New York University, University of North Carolina, University of Southern California, Stanford University, Vanderbilt University, University of Wisconsin and Wayne State University.

The future would be bleak if the richest nation on earth were unable to recruit and support gifted young people in its most vital profession. Public awareness can insure a new era for American education.

For further information about Harvard teacher education programs contact:

Judson T. Shaplin, Associate Dean
Graduate School of Education
Harvard University
3 Lawrence Hall
Kirkland St.
Cambridge 38, Mass.

For related experimental programs see Appendix, pp. 189–91.

Appendix:

RELATED EXPERIMENTAL
PROGRAMS

TEAM TEACHING

NORWALK, CONN. HAS BEEN EXPERI-
menting with team teaching for the past two years. Each
three-person team consists of a team leader, a fully certifi-
cated teacher and an aide. The team conducts classes of
as many as 75–80 students. Classes regroup into smaller
combinations depending upon the subject matter being
taught.

The team leader receives a salary about 15 percent
higher than that of a regular teacher on maximum salary,
the second teacher receives about 5 percent more and the
aide about 20 percent less. Aides are high school graduates
with some college training who have worked with children.
Some have special talents in music and art but their primary duties are clerical.

Four schools have participated in the experiment. The
crossing of grade lines is being explored in 1959–60.

Contact: Mr. Bryce Perkins, Director
THE NORWALK PLAN
Norwalk Board of Education
Magrath School
South Norwalk, Conn.

Milwaukee, Wis. has perhaps the oldest nongraded plan in existence though it is limited to the years between the first and fourth grades. Children begin the primary unit after kindergarten, progressing from P1 at their own rates of speed until ready for the fourth grade which usually occurs after P6. Since 111 of Milwaukee's 113 elementary schools have adopted this plan it involves more children than any other similar program in the country.

Contact: Florence C. Kelly, Director
Division of Primary Curriculum and
  Instruction
Milwaukee Public Schools
1111 N. 10th St.
Milwaukee 1, Wis.

Long Beach and Ossining, N.Y., in connection with the Experimental Teaching Center, School of Education, New York University, are experimenting with a dual progress plan. From the third through the sixth grade pupils spend half the day in graded classes in social studies, language arts and physical education. During the other half of the day students are ability grouped in ungraded classes taught by specialists in mathematics, science, music, arts and crafts.

The theoretical foundations of this plan were developed by Dr. George D. Stoddard of New York University, which has established an Experimental Teaching Center for coordination, research and evaluation of the project.

176

Contacts: Dr. Glen Heathers, Director
             Experimental Teaching Center
             School of Education
             New York University
             Room 520 MAIN
             New York 3, N.Y.

             Dr. Gilbert M. Trachtman
             Research Coordinator
             Long Beach Public School System
             Long Beach, N.Y.

             Mr. David W. Bishop, Study Director
             Ossining Public School System
             Ossining, N.Y.

Torrance, Calif. has developed a multigrade class program combining children from several grade and age levels in one room. It was started at the Walteria School as a result of a doctoral study by Walter Rehwoldt and Warren W. Hamilton and is now in operation in four other schools of the district.

In Walteria, seven "multigraded," "multiage" classes have been organized. The primary classes are made up of first, second and third graders. Intermediate classes consist of fourth, fifth and sixth graders.

The Rehwoldt-Hamilton study indicated generally that children in the multigrade classes made greater gains in achievement, personal adjustment and maturity than children in single grade "control" classes.

The plan has been received with enthusiasm by teachers, students and parents of the schools where it is in operation.

Contact: Dr. A. N. Posner, Assistant Superintendent
Education Services
Torrance Unified School District
2335 Plaza Del Amo
Torrance, Calif.

TEACHER AIDES

New York City School Volunteers, sponsored by the Public Education Association and supported by the Ford Foundation and the New York Fund for Children, have worked in the city's schools for the past four years. They assist teachers in the classroom, help individual children in language arts and enrich the curriculum in music, art and other activities.

Last year 180 volunteers contributed more than 140,000 hours to this program. At the present time 154 volunteers serve in 10 schools.

Contact: T. Margaret Jamer, Director
School Volunteers
125 West 54th St.
New York 19, N.Y.

Newton High School, Newton, Mass., employs women of the community to read and grade compositions written by its English students. Their utilization permits more frequent assignments in the creative writing so lacking in most U.S. high schools.

Six women, all liberal arts graduates with strong backgrounds in English, were chosen after a summer workshop and screening program. They work approximately 250

178

hours a year, 80 of which are spent in student conferences, 170 in correcting the compositions. They receive $2 an hour.

Both Concord (Mass.) High School and Quincy (Mass.) Junior High School have adopted similar programs.

Contact: Dr. Charles E. Brown, Assistant
                Superintendent
                Newton Public Schools
                430 Walnut St.
                Newtonville 60, Mass.

TELEVISION

The New York State Regents Educational Television Project is supported by the New York State Education Department. It transmits lessons over commercial television station WPIX, channel 11, New York, Monday through Friday from 9:50 a.m. to 3 p.m.

Sixty-five programs a week reach a school audience of 450,000. Elementary, secondary and college courses are presented "live" and on film.

The TV teachers are drawn from several New York State school systems and contributors to programming include the National Educational Radio and Television Center, the Museum of Modern Art, St. John's, Columbia and New York universities.

The State Education Department encourages local experimentation and evaluation and extends necessary assistance as requested.

Contact: James F. Macandrew, Executive Director
                Regents Educational Television Project
                220 East 42d St., Tenth Floor
                New York 17, N.Y.

Schools of Tomorrow—Today!

Cortland (*N.Y.*) Public Schools and those of Truxton and Virgil are benefiting from closed-circuit educational television cosponsored by the New York State Education Department.

Eight buildings are linked by 25 miles of cable encompassing 3 separate school systems with 45 classrooms and 3,000 students.

The project includes a talk-back facility which permits the teacher on camera as well as students in any classroom to communicate with each other when necessary.

In the elementary schools, courses in science, health, music, language arts, writing, reading, arithmetic and citizenship education are being offered in the school year 1959–60, the second year of the project. On the high school level, courses in music, mathematics and health are offered.

The television circuit has also been utilized to carry special news and current events programs, citywide faculty meetings, PTA programs, adult education courses and special on-the-spot programs for students of various grades.

    Contact: Raymond Graf, TV Director
                   Closed Circuit Project
                   Munson Corners School
                   Cortland, N.Y.

THE GIFTED CHILD

The National Education Association's Project on the Academically Talented Student is directed by Dr. Charles E. Bish and supported by the Carnegie Corporation of New York. It has a three-fold purpose. It serves as a clearing house of information and its files include thousands of examples of programs for the academically talented from all parts of the United States. Secondly, it provides a consulting service for which Dr. Bish has visited 60 areas during the past year. Its third function is to arrange conferences with professional organizations and disseminate informational materials. It publishes a bulletin, *The Clearing-House*. Other pamphlets, including *Science for the Academically Talented* and *Math for the Academically Talented* are available upon request.

Contact: Dr. Charles Bish, Director
Project on the Academically Talented
Student
National Education Association
1201 16th St., NW
Washington 6, D.C.

The North Central Association of Colleges and Secondary Schools has embarked on an ambitious program financed by the Carnegie Corporation of New York.

The NCA is a voluntary regional accrediting association composed of 3,500 high schools and 419 colleges and universities in 19 States.

This project, designed to improve practices for identifying, guiding and motivating superior and talented students, is being carried on in 100 of these high schools. It involves some 18,000 selected students and is being conducted by a full-time staff with Science Research Associates as consultants.

Contact: J. Ned Bryan, Director
NCA STS Project
57 West Grand Ave.
Chicago 10, Ill.

Schools of Tomorrow—Today!

The Portland (*Oreg.*) Public School System, incooperation with Reed College, has developed a comprehensive districtwide plan for the identification and development of the talented child. Starting as a five-year experiment (1952–57) under a grant from the Fund for the Advancement of Education, the program now is an integral part of the city school system. It is in operation in 55 elementary schools and 10 high schools.

A coordinator in each school building spends half of each day working on the program. Teachers receive in-service training and attend summer workshops.

The program for the gifted varies in each school. On the elementary level, regular class programs are enriched. In the seventh and eighth grades there are special classes for gifted students in such subjects as arithmetic, science, language arts, foreign language and art. These meet two to five times a week.

In high school talented students may take advanced work in regular courses during all four years. Seminars in subject areas are offered in the junior-senior years.

Contact: Clifford W. Williams, Director
Gifted Child Project
Portland Public Schools
631 Northeast Clackamas St.
Portland 8, Oreg.

Cleveland (*Ohio*) Public Schools have long provided a system for early identification and grouping of the academically gifted. More than 35 centers located in school buildings are designated for students of superior ability with IQs of 125 and above. In addition, there are enrichment classes at other centers for above-average students.

About 2,000 of Cleveland's 129,000 elementary and secondary students participate in this program. Under the supervision of specially trained teachers these students expand their horizons in a rich program designed for their unique abilities.

Contact: Dorothy E. Norris
           Directing Supervisor of Major Work Classes
           Cleveland Public Schools
           Cleveland, Ohio

The Archdiocese of Louisville, Ky., inaugurated a Junior Great Books Program for eighth graders which now extends from the 5th through the 12th grade.

Groups of 15 students meet twice a month to analyze an assigned book. Discussions are conducted by leaders with B.A. degrees who have completed a summer training program.

Fifteen books are covered each year.

Contact: Rt. Rev. Msgr. F. N. Pitt
           Secretary, Catholic School Board
           Archdiocese of Louisville
           151 South Fifth St.
           Louisville 2, Ky.

The Westminster Schools of Atlanta, Ga., are conducting an eight-year experiment (1954–62) to enrich curriculum and link more effectively the last two years of high school with the first two years of college. These independent schools have worked out cooperative programs with Agnes Scott College, Oglethorpe and Emory universities. Elements of the program have been adopted by the Atlanta Public Schools.

The curriculum at the Westminster Schools is enriched from the 1st through the 12th grades.

Contact: William L. Pressley, President
The Westminster Schools
3210 Howell Mill Road, NW
Atlanta, Ga.

San Angelo (Tex.) Public Schools have developed separate curriculums for gifted, average and slower learners from the 1st through the 12th grades.

Experimental programs include flexible scheduling and innovations in teacher utilization (multiple classes, teacher aides, teaching teams, variations in class size).

The program is financed partially by the Fund for the Advancement of Education with increasing support from the San Angelo Board of Education.

Contact: G. B. Wadzeck, Superintendent of Schools
244 North Magdalen
San Angelo, Tex.

SUMMER PROGRAMS FOR GIFTED STUDENTS

The National Science Foundation is an independent agency of the Federal Government supporting basic research, education in science and improved interchange of information.

In 1959 it initiated summer programs designed to encourage scientific interest among high ability secondary school students by enabling them to use college and university facilities. Their advanced work is supervised by faculty members. They participate in research, working alongside experienced scientists in advanced laboratory investigations.

In the summer of 1960 the National Science Foundation will make grants amounting to about $1,880,000 for programs involving over 6,000 high school students who will attend approximately 108 colleges, universities and non-profit research organizations throughout the country.

Financial support by the foundation may cover direct and indirect costs to the participating institutions and as much as 50 percent of the cost of room, board and travel for students.

Contact: Project Director for Summer Science Training Program for Secondary School Students

Special Projects in Science Education Section

Division of Scientific Personnel and Education

National Science Foundation

Washington 25, D.C.

The Rockefeller Institute in New York City offers an eight-week program in college-level science and laboratory work for a selected number of able high school seniors. The courses are conducted by talented graduate students of the institute.

The program, initiated by Detlev W. Bronk, institute president, under a grant from the Carnegie Corporation of New York, has two goals. It is designed to inspire scientific interest among talented high school graduates and to stimulate interest in teaching among outstanding graduate students. Principals of selected high schools nominate all candidates.

Contact: Douglas Whitaker
Vice President for Administration
The Rockefeller Institute
New York 21, N.Y.

St. Paul's School, Concord, N.H., conducts a six-week summer program for able high school students from throughout the State. In collaboration with the State Department of Education, the Advanced Studies Program offers courses normally not available to these students including Latin, Greek, modern languages, science, mathematics, English and history.

The program enables high school teachers to learn more about teaching the gifted and recruits college students as teacher aides or interns in an effort to stimulate candidates for the teaching profession.

Contact: Rev. Matthew M. Warren
St. Paul's School
Concord, N.H.

Thayer Academy, in cooperation with Greater Boston universities and industrial firms, conducts a 10-week research apprenticeship program for advance study in biology, physics, chemistry and mathematics for sixty able secondary school students who have completed their junior year. It is directed jointly by university scientists and school science teachers.

Contact: Gordon O. Thayer, Headmaster
Thayer Academy
Braintree, Mass.

The University of Louisville, Louisville, Ky., in cooperation with the city county high schools and under a grant from the Carnegie Corporation, offers a 10-week summer course to talented high school juniors. College freshman credit courses are offered in science, mathematics, economics, English, history and the humanities.

Priority is given to those able juniors who would not ordinarily enter college because of financial reasons or lack of family interest.

Contact: J. J. Oppenheimer, Coordinator
Summer Scholarship Program
College of Arts and Sciences
University of Louisville
Louisville, Ky.

The Texas Education Agency and a number of Texas schools and colleges conduct five-week summer programs in science and mathematics for talented high school students. The first was held at the University of Texas in 1956.

In addition to encouraging the able student to advance his knowledge the summer programs strengthen his eligibility for college scholarships.

Contact: Dr. L. D. Haskew
Vice President for Development Services
University of Texas
Austin 12, Tex.

IMPROVEMENT OF RURAL SCHOOLS

The Rocky Mountain Area Project for Small High Schools is a three-year experiment (1957–60) initiated by the Colorado State Department of Education with a grant from the Fund for the Advancement of Education. It is designed to develop more effective use of teachers' time in small high schools and to explore patterns of organization uniquely applicable to schools of this size.

Techniques employed include multiple classes (one teacher conducting two or more related courses simultaneously within one classroom), the use of teacher aides, supervised correspondence courses and shared seminar programs for capable students, small group meetings and the use of audio tape, filmed courses and recordings.

At present eighteen high schools participate in the project.

Contact: Ralph G. Bohrson, Director
            Rocky Mountain Area Project
            Department of Education
            Denver 2, Colo.

Lewis County, N.Y., holds a weekly seminar for able students from five rural high schools. The students tackle one major problem during the year. Many disciplines are brought to bear on such topics as *The Nature of Freedom, Man and Change,* and *Communications.*

Contact: Dr. Glyn Morris, Assistant Superintendent
            Board of Cooperative Educational Services
                for Lewis County
            Lyons Falls, N.Y.

Goddard College of Plainfield, Vt., originated a program in 1956 to assist rural schools. Students with special skills serve as teacher assistants in these schools.

They supplement the regular teachers' instruction and,

when qualified, take over total instruction in such fields as art, music, physical education and science.

This work, for which the student can gain credit, may constitute one-third of his college program. The experiment has served to improve the education of rural children and stimulate the interest of future teachers. Several other colleges in Vermont and Maine are sponsoring similar programs.

Contact: President Royce Pitkin
Goddard College
Plainfield, Vt.

TEACHER RECRUITMENT

Flint (Mich.) Public Schools in conjunction with Central Michigan University and the Mott Foundation Program of Flint's Board of Education recruit able high school graduates for teacher training.

The Mott Foundation provides scholarship assistance when needed and an "earn while you learn" feature makes a teaching career feasible financially for students who could otherwise not afford higher education.

The five-year program begins with two years of basic college training at the Flint Community Junior College. This is followed by three years of earning-learning, split between supervised teaching in the Flint schools and classes at Central Michigan University.

Contact: Spencer W. Myers, Superintendent
Flint Public Schools
Flint, Mich.

Schools of Tomorrow—Today!

The Yale-Fairfield Study of Elementary Teaching has conducted four experiments in recruitment, training and utilization of elementary school teachers.

In one experiment, eight young mothers, all liberal arts graduates, were selected for a three-year teacher training program. This was carried out by the College of Education of the University of Bridgeport and the Fairfield (Conn.) School System.

The recruits attended seminars in teacher education for five semesters. They spent at least three hours a week in the classroom as observers and as teacher aides. During the last semester there was a six-week period of practice teaching.

At the completion of the program the women had earned 30 semester hours of graduate credit and were granted provisional teaching certificates.

Five of the eight mothers are still on the job. They are regarded as superior to the average beginning teacher.

Contact: Dr. Clyde M. Hill, Director
Yale-Fairfield Study of Elementary Teaching
Yale University
New Haven, Conn.

Alexander Ramsey High School, St. Paul, Minn., includes a teacher orientation program for interested students as part of its social studies course for seniors.

Students act as teacher assistants 4 hours a week for 12 weeks. Each works with teachers at two grade levels. Classes in general psychology supplement the experience.

Fifteen of the 31 students who participated in the teacher orientation program of 1955 have completed teacher education requirements in four-year colleges.

Contact: Dr. Robert J. Swan, Director
Pupil Personnel Services
Roseville Schools
St. Paul, Minn.

THE NEW TECHNOLOGY

Mount Saint Scholastica College, Atchison, Kans., has pioneered in the development of teaching by magnetic tape at primary, secondary and college levels.

The college has created a library of taped lessons for use in "electronic classrooms" equipped with recording and playback apparatus.

Three-channel tape curriculum enables students of varying abilities to receive lectures simultaneously in the same classroom. Wearing earphones they hear only their own lesson and can communicate directly with the teacher.

Mount Saint Scholastica has experimented in the use of magnetic discs and tapes for instruction in foreign languages.

A number of schools are utilizing these materials and summer workshops at the college have spread knowledge of tape techniques.

Contact: Sister Mary Theresa, OSB
Mount St. Scholastica College
Atchison, Kans.

#3067230